DISCOVERING MUSIC

Student Workbook

Second Edition

Carol B. Reynolds, Ph.D.

with

M. Fletcher Reynolds, Ph.D.

Silver Age Music, Inc.

© 2022 by Silver Age Music, Inc.

All rights reserved. No part of this book may be reproduced or transmitted in any form or by any means, electronic or mechanical, including photocopying, recording, or by any information storage and retrieval system, without permission in writing from the Publisher.

Silver Age Music, Inc.
P.O. Box 85
Bethania, NC 27010

PRINTED IN THE UNITED STATES OF AMERICA

ISBN: 978-1-7345956-3-5

040822

Table of Contents

How To Use this Workbook 4

Key Dates 10

Three Mega Composers 17

Unit 1: Using Music History To Unlock Western Culture 18

Unit 2: Music Entwined with Great Events in Western History 35

Unit 3: Technology, Terminology, and Cultural Perspective 45

Unit 4: Fanfare and Power: The Court of Louis XIV 51

Unit 5: Sweeping Away the Renaissance into the Baroque 61

Unit 6: Liturgical Calendar, Street Parties, and the New Church Music 71

Unit 7: A Lively Journey Through the Life of Johann Sebastian Bach 79

Unit 8: Enlightenment, Classicism, and the Astonishing Mozart 88

Unit 9: Into the Abyss: The Century Struggles with Unfettered Imagination 99

Unit 10: Beethoven as Hero and Revolutionary 109

Unit 11: Salons, Poetry, and the Power of Song 117

Unit 12: A Tale of Four Virtuosi and the Birth of the Tone Poem 125

Unit 13: Nationalism and the Explosion of Romantic Opera 136

Unit 14: The Absolutely New World of Wagner 149

Unit 15: Imperial Russia – A Cultural Odyssey 157

Unit 16: Load Up the Wagons: The Story of American Music 170

Uniti 17: Turning the Page on Western Tradition with the Explosion of War 181

QUIZZES 193

SUGGESTED ANSWERS FOR VIEWING GUIDES 210

Listening Form 223

How To Use this Workbook

This book is designed to serve as a companion to the *Discovering Music Video Lectures* and the *Discovering Music Text*. The complete course includes this Student Workbook, a separate Textbook, and 17 Video Lectures contained on an 8 DVD set.

All listening selections can be found online:

www.professorcarol.com/dm-listening

Additional supporting materials are online:

www.professorcarol.com/dm-supplement

Each unit of the course is constructed to present the music of a particular cultural era, phenomenon, or composer. Rather than attempt a comprehensive history of Western Art Music (what is often loosely labeled "Classical"), this course seeks to introduce and analyze significant musical developments within the social, historical, and cultural contexts that fostered them. The premise is simply this: music, or any creative product, does not occur in a vacuum. It is more often the outpouring of education, training, priorities, and values of human beings. Even the most intimidating music has often come about for the most practical—even *humble*—of reasons! Understanding these reasons can change completely how we perceive this art.

Discovering Music seeks to present music in its "original habitat," historically speaking. Our hope is that gaining an understanding of this habitat, along with a greater awareness of music's interaction with the fields of literature, visual art, history, and technology, will equip students for a wealth of musical experiences. And this understanding will be a powerful tool to unlock academics, culture, and history.

The Figures (People), Places, and Dates chosen for each unit are intended to provide students with "hooks"—concrete pieces of information that will offer a foundation of historical knowledge or additional historical perspective, depending upon a student's age or grade level. The Vocabulary sections are intended to supplement and support terms or concepts presented in the Video Lectures. The Listening Selections presented for each unit are provided as guides to further listening for the most significant composers or genres presented within each unit.

PEOPLE

The initial building block of each unit is a list of the historical figures that appear most prominently in the context of the unit. The lists include composers, relevant political figures, scientists, philosophers, authors, artists, and performers. Nearly every name will be mentioned specifically within the Video Lectures. Others may be mentioned only in the Text. Those few listed but not mentioned are useful to the unit's topic and can be researched separately. You may wish to do some or all of the following:

- incorporate some (or all!) of these figures into a timeline
- select certain individuals whom you wish to study in more depth
- research individuals relevant to your studies in other subject areas
- search for resources (books, movies, documentaries, etc.) on these individuals at your local library

PLACES

Most units contain a list of relevant geographical locations. Students should be able to locate these places on a map. In this Second Edition, coordinates are provided in many cases so that the student can pinpoint the location and visit it online with Google Earth or a similar application. The student may also wish to research the history of a particular city or even a broader geographical region. Although the scope of this course necessitates certain limits, students will notice that many places—for instance, Paris or Vienna—appear repeatedly and could easily fill a unit by themselves!

VOCABULARY

These definitions are intended to reinforce and clarify the information presented in the course materials. A brief explanation of important terms can be found in the Glossary contained in the Text. The definitions provided are not intended to replace the student's consultation of a good dictionary or encyclopedia. Because so many musical and cultural terms are in foreign languages, take advantage of the translations and explanations provided; many times, when encountering a term in a foreign language, it is helpful just to be able to "see" the word in print and associate the pronunciations in the lecture with the way a word looks on the page.

Be sure to know all vocabulary words and their definitions prior to taking the Unit Quizzes.

DATES

One of the most effective ways to learn and retain history is through developing associations. The Timelines presented in each unit attempt to place the topics within a particular historical setting. Please note: these sections are NOT designed to outline any one composer's biography or to give a complete picture of any era of history. We urge you to make your own timelines wherever possible. You may also wish to do some or all of the following:

- select certain major events from this section to memorize
- incorporate some (or all!) of these events into a grand timeline that covers the

entire period of the course

- perform additional research on specific battles, discoveries, inventions, or other historical events

LISTENING

Choosing listening selections for the course is one of the chief challenges we faced in creating the course *Discovering Music.* We are only too aware of the endless possibilities that could have been included! Happily, it has become comparatively easy, in our modern day, to access music online.

In our original edition of this course, we included a set of audio discs. In this second edition, we have replaced that part of the course with online resources. We made this change somewhat reluctantly after concluding that the benefits of having a physical CD set were outweighed by the limitations.

So now you will find Listening Selections for each Unit plus links to online performances in the Online Listening Guide (www.professorcarol.com/dm-listening). This solution allows us to keep the list up to date and to include many more selections for exploring the repertoire. You should listen to each of these works, preferably more than once. A Listening Form is included in the Appendix to this Workbook to help keep students on track and listening effectively with particular goals.

You may also wish to do some or all of the following:

- listen to all of the remaining movements of a multi-movement work
- find and listen to additional works by a composer who catches your interest
- concentrate on a particular genre that appeals to you (concerto, symphony, arias, choruses, etc.)
- determine which types of instrumental or vocal sounds appeal to you
- find music of other composers who were writing during the same time and in a similar style

ONLINE RESOURCES

Additional materials related to each of the units can be found online at www.professorcarol.com/dm-supplemental. In some cases, these materials may include artworks and additional online videos.

Parents, please note: We have taken care to keep the materials presented in this course family-friendly and age-appropriate. However, a great deal of art history revolves around depictions of the human body. As you know, artists must learn to sketch, draw, paint, and sculpt the body. Please be aware that many art websites may show figures in ways that those concerned about this aspect of art may wish to avoid. As students explore the art under discussion on other websites, especially as the course progresses closer into and through the 19th century, students are more likely to encounter mature materials. Be assured, though, that students will not encounter nude images in our course materials.

PUTTING IT ALL TOGETHER

Most units contain a section called "Putting It All Together." The questions and projects listed in this section are a guide to synthesizing the information presented. Depending on the student's grade level and level of interest, you may wish to choose one activity per unit or you may attempt more, based on the student's needs and interests. The student is also invited to create projects based on individual interests.

Your selection of projects is a primary tool in tailoring the course to a student's grade level. Some projects are well suited to groups of students working together. Some can be adapted to very young ages. Others can be intensified to reach college-level research. Read through the questions and projects in this section before beginning your research. In addition to online resources, students are encouraged to use traditional research materials as well (e.g. encyclopedias, magazine articles, and biographies) to gather relevant information for a given project.

Projects generally fall into three categories:

Academic Research. These projects require traditional research methods involving library or internet reference materials, formal writing techniques, footnotes or endnotes, and the compilation of a bibliography.

Comparative Analysis. Students will seek out and familiarize themselves with a variety of new materials and resources, and then draw comparisons and contrasts.

Field Research. Students will go "out into the field" and see how music and the arts apply within the institutions that make up their communities.

VIEWING GUIDES

To get the most out of *Discovering Music*, we recommend watching each video lecture two times. Viewing Guides are drawn entirely from the lectures and are designed to help students learn to take notes and keep track of the most relevant information while viewing the video lectures. Therefore, we encourage the student first to view the videos without the Viewing Guide, ideally taking notes, and then use the Viewing Guide in one of two ways: (1) as a review, working through it after viewing the video lecture to see how much information can be recalled, or (2) as an outline to be filled in during a second viewing of the lecture. The Viewing Guides may also serve as a more advanced unit quiz for some students. Suggested answers are given in the back of this Workbook, including multiple answers where appropriate.

UNIT QUIZZES AND EXAMS

The Unit Quiz for each chapter is found in the back of the Workbook. The quiz is deliberately kept very basic, but it draws from all sections of the unit material. Answers are provided in the Online Teacher's Manual (see below), including multiple answers where needed. But keep in mind that, in many cases, additional answers can be correct. Describing music and the arts is not an exact science. Students may wish to design their own unit quizzes. It's excellent academic practice to do so!

The course includes four rather rigorous exams for students taking the course for credit. The exams are to be taken at the end of Units 6, 10, 14, and 17. These exams are also provided in the Online Teacher's Manual.

The **Online Teacher's Manual** is available for download at www.professorcarol.com/professor-carols-store. In order to keep the exam questions secure, we have opted to make them available only by download and at the nominal price of $1.00. If this presents a problem, please let us know and we will make efforts to accommodate you.

Video Timings

Disc 1
Unit 1	Using Music History to Unlock Western Culture	44:56
Unit 2	Music Entwined with Great Events in Western History	41:56
Unit 3	Technology, Terminology, and Cultural Perspective	25.35

Disc 2
Unit 4	Fanfare and Power: The Court of Louis XIV	34:01
Unit 5	Sweeping Away the Renaissance into the Baroque	48.18
Unit 6	Liturgical Calendar, Street Parties, and the New Church Music	27:31

Disc 3
Unit 7	A Lively Journey through the Life of Johann Sebastian Bach	50:56
Unit 8	Enlightenment, Classicism, and the Astonishing Mozart	58:26

Disc 4
Unit 9	Into the Abyss: The Century Struggles with Unfettered Imagination	58:06
Unit 10	Beethoven as Hero and Revolutionary	37:48

Disc 5
Unit 11	Salons, Poetry, and the Power of Song	49:07
Unit 12	A Tale of Four Virtuosi and the Birth of the Tone Poem	53:09

Disc 6
Unit 13	Nationalism and the Explosion of Romantic Opera	56:05
Unit 14	The Absolutely New World of Wagner	35:48

Disc 7
Unit 15	Imperial Russia PA Cultural Odyssey	58:35
Unit 16	Load Up the Wagons: The Story of American Music	1:01:36

Disc 8
Unit 17	Turning the Page on Western Tradition with the Explosion of War	1:00:43

Total time: 13:22:36

Key Dates

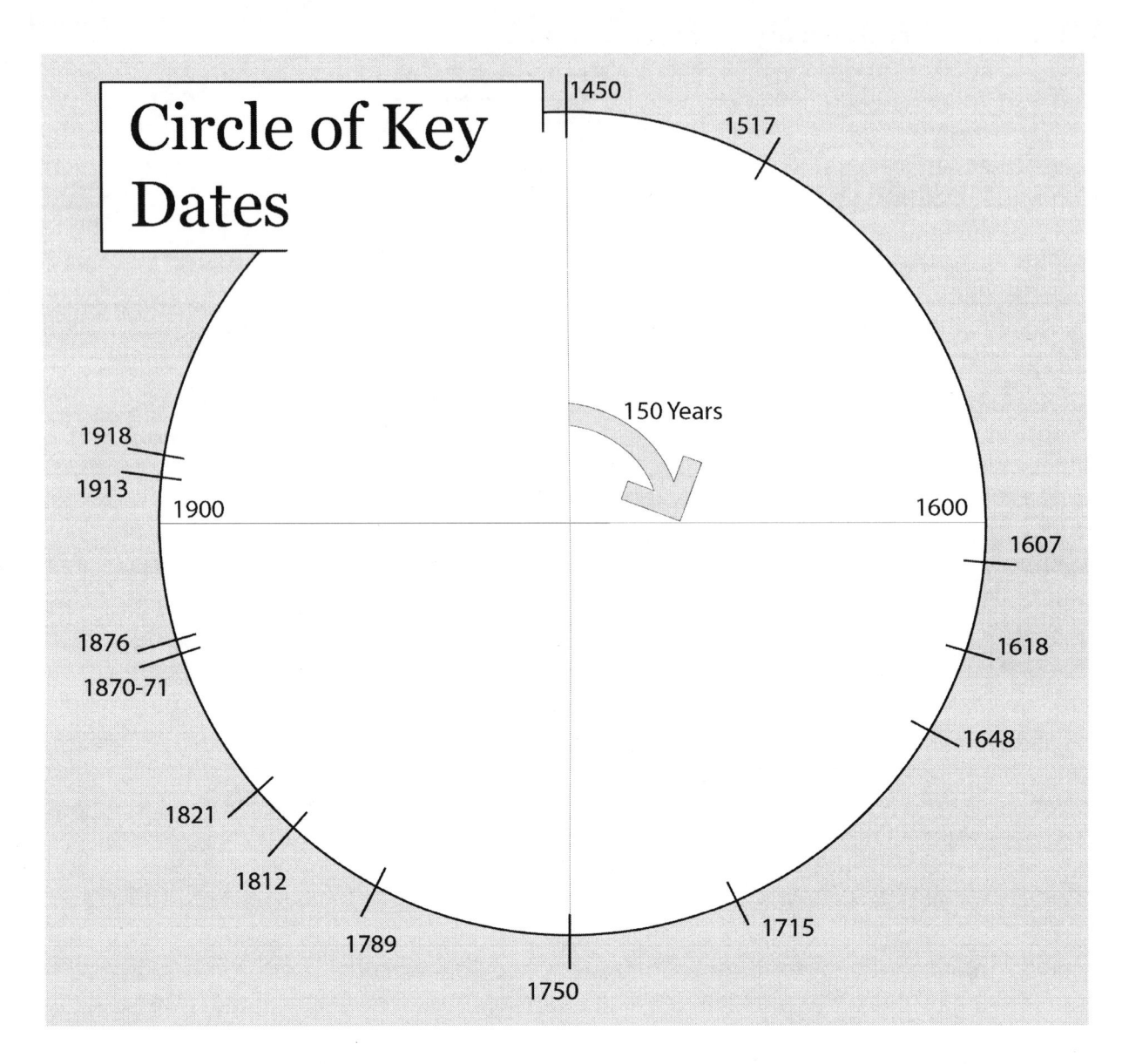

Circle of Key Dates

- 1450
- 1517
- 1600
- 1607
- 1618
- 1648
- 1715
- 1750
- 1789
- 1812
- 1821
- 1870-71
- 1876
- 1900
- 1913
- 1918

150 Years

Key to the Circle of Dates

1450   A good general date for the beginning of the printing press. Gutenberg, working in the German city of Mainz, had been developing his press for years, but he made significant advances in typography in 1450. These advances laid the groundwork for printing a series of Bibles known as the Gutenberg Bibles.

Key Dates

1517	On October 31, a monk named Martin Luther nailed the 95 Theses, or 95 statements of theological protest, to the door of the Wittenberg Cathedral, intending to address abuses, but ultimately setting the split between the Roman Catholic and new Protestants (Protestant Reformation) into motion.
1607	Claudio Monteverdi's opera *Orfeo*. It is the earliest opera still regularly produced. Considered a landmark in the development of Baroque style, it is heavily rooted in Renaissance musical and theatrical traditions.
1618-1648	The Thirty Years' War. The bloody struggle to determine whether Europe would remain Catholic or become Protestant. In the end, the Southern regions primarily retained the traditional Catholic faith, and Northern areas turned primarily Protestant. Since the war lasted 30 years, these are easy dates to learn.
1715	Death of the Sun King, Louis XIV. His descendants continued to build the palace of Versailles, and to nourish French artist life, but nothing matched the personal and dynastic glitter of Louis XIV's court.
1750	Death of Johann Sebastian Bach.
1789	The French Revolution begins. All European monarchs are "put on notice."
1812	Napoleon's defeat in Russia (many of his famished troops froze during their retreat back to France). The Battle of Waterloo three years later (1815) resulted in the final defeat of Napoleon.
1821	Premiere of Carl Maria von Weber's *Der Freischütz*, or The Free Shot. It was not the first German-language spoken-dialogue opera or even the first opera based on magic (after all, Mozart's *The Magic Flute* in 1791 qualifies on both accounts). But *Der Freischütz* offered authentic German folk music and wove German folklore and legend together. It also featured the trendy "spooky" elements, including the "Wolf's Glen Scene" that can send a shiver down one's spine.

1870-1871	The Franco-Prussian War, the first great modern clash between the French and the Germans. The Germans won, and thoroughly humiliated the French with insufferable peace terms. The treaty was signed in the Hall of Mirrors at Versailles, which was a further slap in France's face. The momentum from this victory led the Germans finally to unite their many regions, kingdoms, bishoprics, and free trade cities into a unified nation, with a central government, and a constitution. From this point on, it's possible to refer to the German nation or the country of Germany, i.e. Deutschland. Otto von Bismarck, known as The Iron Chancellor, was the master diplomat whose name emerged from this period. His clever strategies kept Europe at peace for decades.
1876	The first performance of all four of Wagner's operas constituting *The Ring*—his famous tetralogy of operas. This performance in August inaugurated Wagner's completely original and innovative new theater, the *Festspielhaus* in the German city of Bayreuth. It was attended by famous people, including Tchaikovsky. Today, the summer festival of Wagner's operas at Bayreuth is a major cultural event.
1913	The premiere of one of the most radical pieces of music ever written, a ballet on a primitive Russian theme by Igor Stravinsky called *The Rite of Spring*. Its premiere in Paris was famously marked by audience protests. The innovative young choreographer who designed this ballet, Vaslav Nijinsky, is still famous to this day for the complex, strange new movements he taught the dancers.
1914-1918	The official dates of World War I, pitting Germany and her allies against France and her allies, ultimately including the United States. Germany was defeated, stripped of territory, and of what few resources remained after the devastating war. The peace treaty was signed in June 1919, again in the Palace of Versailles—an inversion of the situation at the end of the Franco-Prussian War.

Key Dates 13

Create your own Circle of Key Dates

- Artistic events
- Military or other world events
- Other significant events

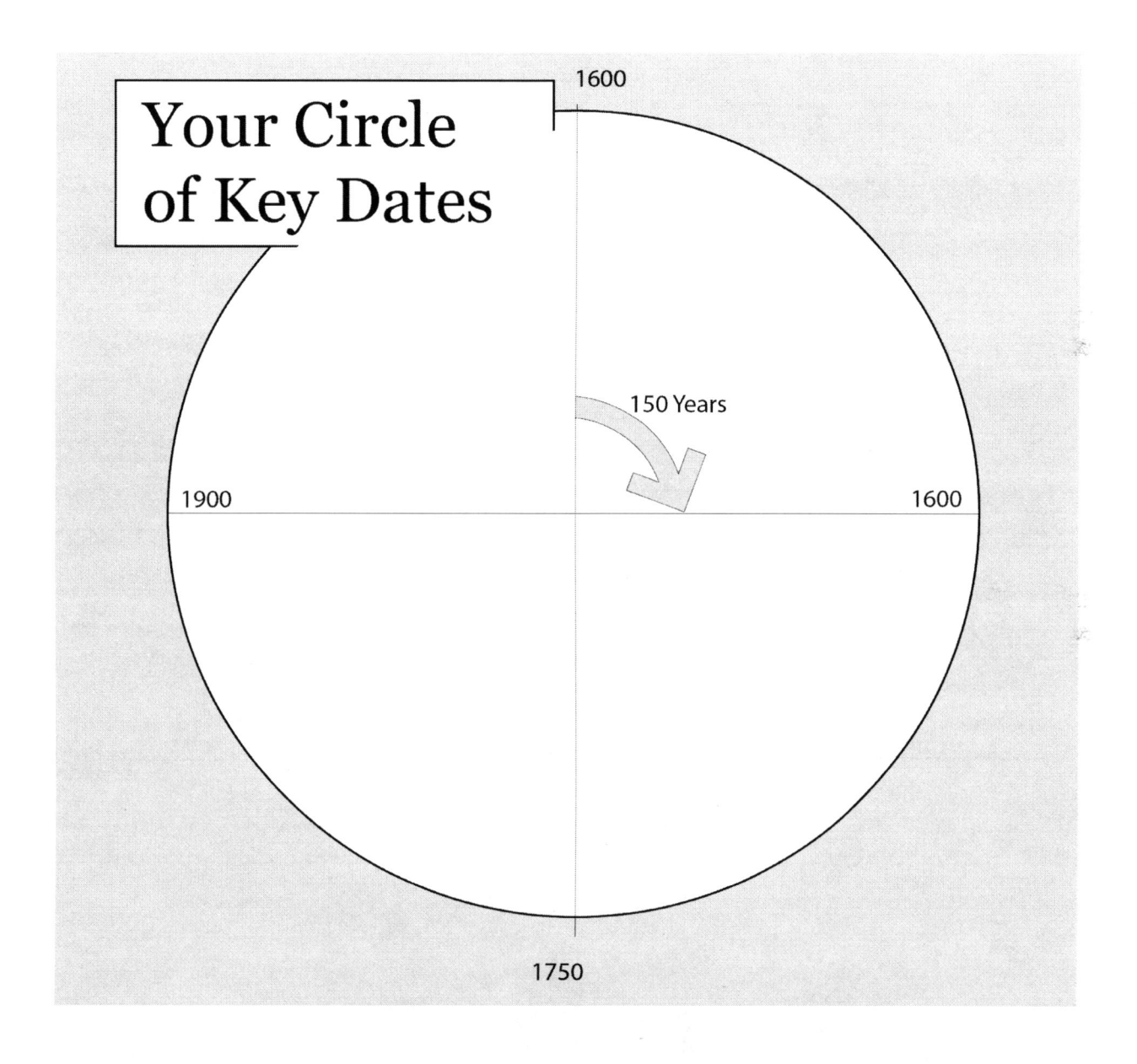

Your Circle of Key Dates

1600

1900

150 Years

1600

1750

Major Eras of Music History

ANCIENT — 600 BC - 410
The Western world flourishes under Greek philosophy and is unified under Roman rule.

Medieval — 410-1400
After the fall of Rome, the Church becomes the main repository of knowledge and education.

Renaissance — 1350-1600
The arts flourish with the rediscovery of Greek philosophy, literature in the vernacular, perspective in painting, and polyphony in music.

Baroque — 1600-1740
The common practice era in begins. Music has a developed tonal system. Opera and oratorio become favorite forms.

Classical — 1740-1820
Order and symmetry characterize the Enlightenment and its confidence in man's perfectability.

Romantic — 1804-1913
The upheavals of revolution and war usher in uncertain times, an age of individualism and secularism.

Alternate View

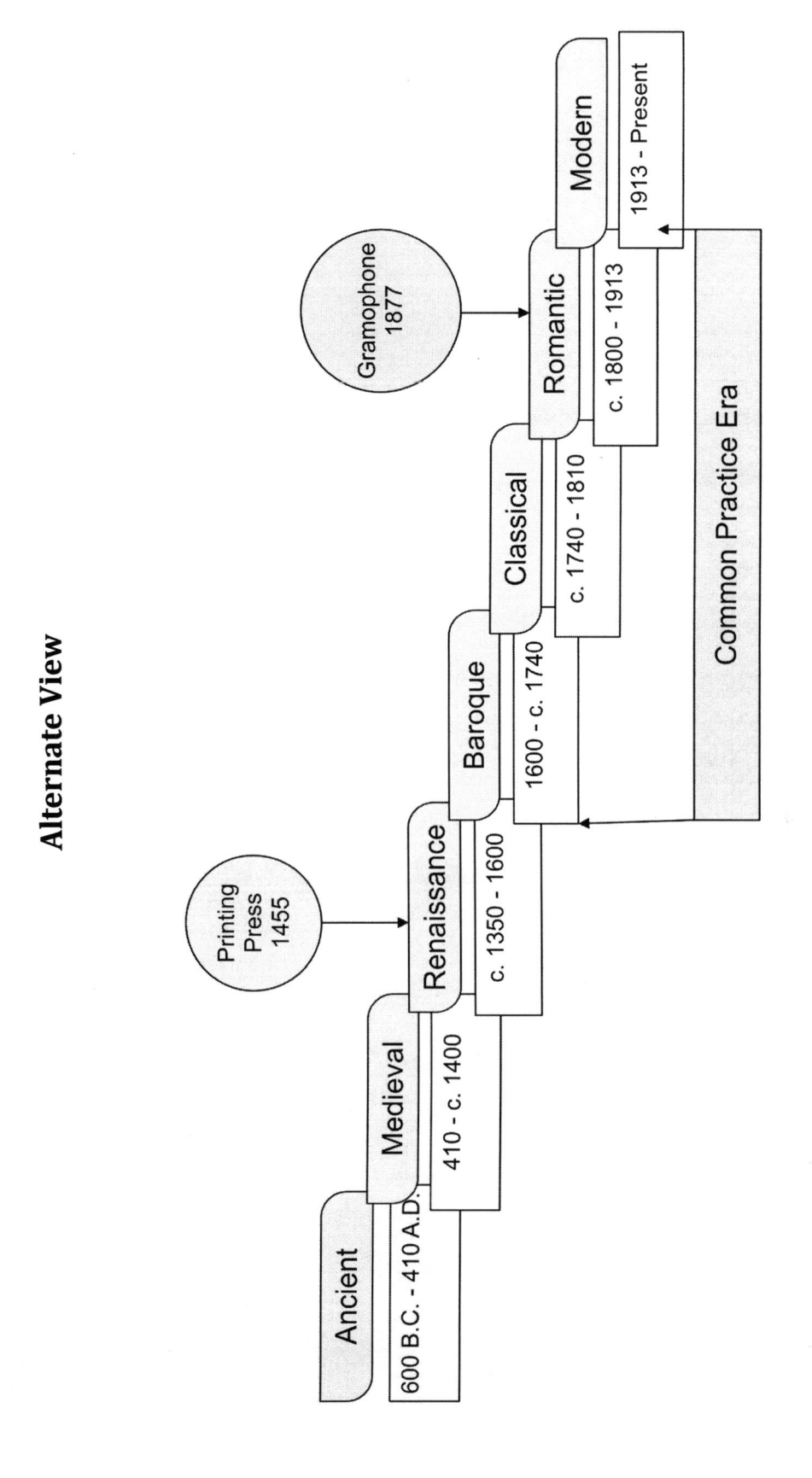

Ancient
600 B.C. – 410 A.D.

Medieval
410 – c. 1400

Printing Press 1455 →

Renaissance
c. 1350 – 1600

Baroque
1600 – c. 1740

Classical
c. 1740 – 1810

Gramophone 1877 →

Romantic
c. 1800 – 1913

Modern
1913 – Present

Common Practice Era

16 DISCOVERING MUSIC STUDENT WORKBOOK

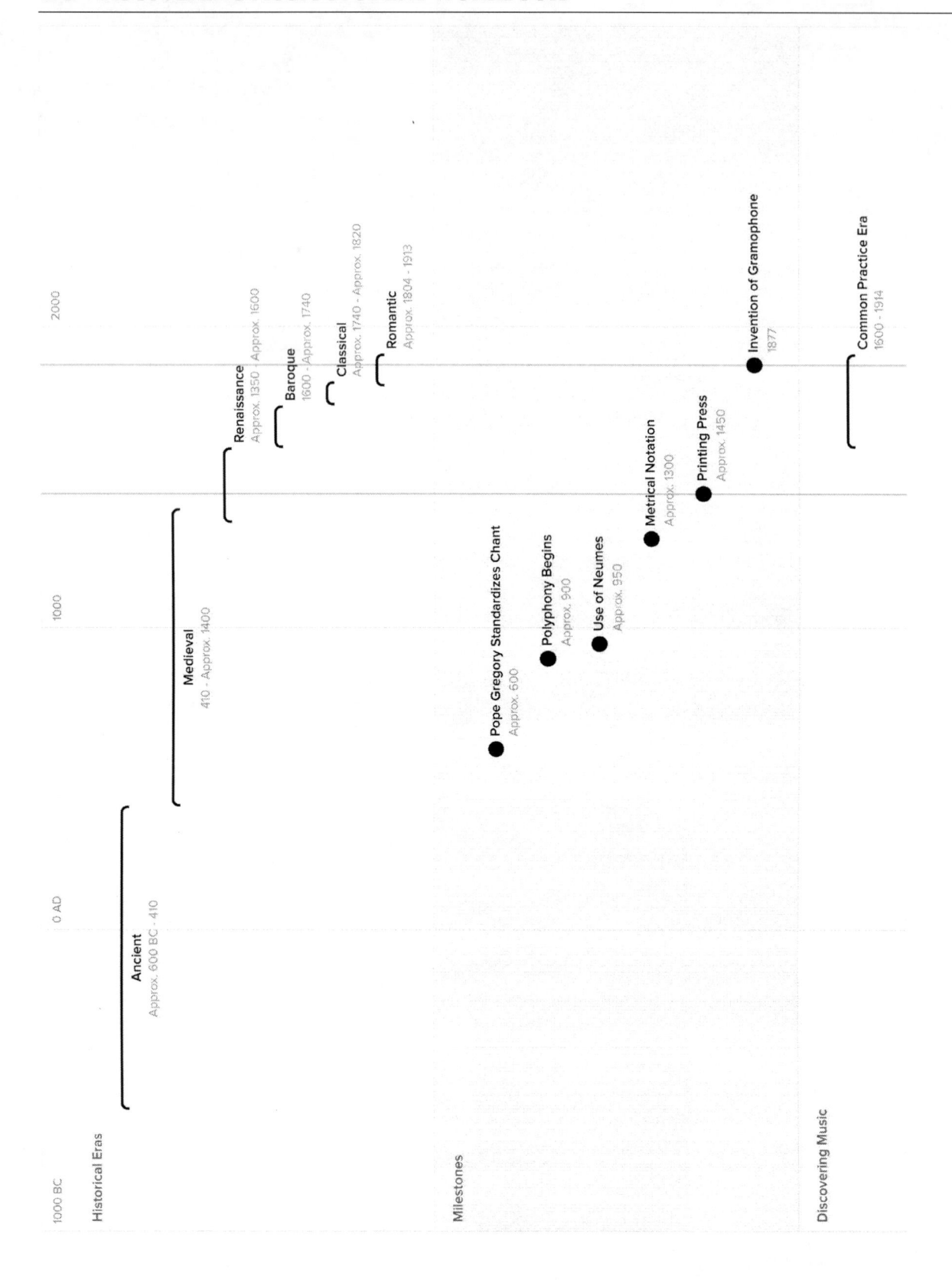

Historical Eras

- **Ancient** — Approx. 600 BC - 410
- **Medieval** — 410 - Approx. 1400
- **Renaissance** — Approx. 1350 - Approx. 1600
- **Baroque** — 1600 - Approx. 1740
- **Classical** — Approx. 1740 - Approx. 1820
- **Romantic** — Approx. 1804 - 1913

Milestones

- **Pope Gregory Standardizes Chant** — Approx. 600
- **Polyphony Begins** — Approx. 900
- **Use of Neumes** — Approx. 950
- **Metrical Notation** — Approx. 1300
- **Printing Press** — Approx. 1450
- **Invention of Gramophone** — 1877

Discovering Music

- **Common Practice Era** — 1600 - 1914

Timeline markers: 1000 BC, 0 AD, 1000, 2000

Three Mega Composers

Bach
Johann Sebastian
1685-1750
Baroque

Germany
Composer

Themes:

Late Baroque Style
Church Music
Cantatas, Chorales, and Oratorios
Organs and Technology
Life as Kapellmeister

Mozart
Wolfgang Amadeus
1756-1791
Classical

Austria
Composer

Themes:

Classical Style
Enlightenment Ideals
Italian Training
Fortepiano
Opera

Beethoven
Ludwig
1770-1827
Classical/Romantic

Germany, Austria
Composer

Themes:

Romanticism and Revolution
Struggle for Individual Expression
Rise of Napoleon
Heiligenstadt Testament
Goethe

Unit 1

Using Music History To Unlock Western Culture

PEOPLE

Plato
c. 427-c. 347 B.C.
Ancient

Greece
Philosopher

Edison
Thomas
1847-1931
Romantic

United States
Inventor

Schumann
Robert
1810-1856
Romantic

Germany
Composer

Schumann
Clara Wieck
1819-1896
Romantic

Germany
Pianist, Composer

John, Paul, George, Ringo
Active 1962-1970
England

The Beatles

PLACES

| Queens Peak, Montague County, Texas | 33°37'35.85" N 97°52'09.24" W |

LISTENING

See Listening Guide at http://www.professorcarol.com/dm-listening

The Listening Selections for Unit 1 explore a variety of styles from widely diverse periods of history.

VOCABULARY

Ears, Brains, Imagination
A phrase you'll hear several times in the course of this study. Each is needed to understand and make use of music (and cultural) history.

45 rpm
A flat recording disc that rotated (spun) 45 times per minute. It held approximately 3 minutes of sound.

iPod
A device for playing "media" (songs, movies) developed and marketed by Apple Inc. and launched in 2001.

Score
The written-down version of musical notes.

Song
A piece of music with words meant to be sung. Songs ordinarily begin with the words (text) and, hence, a phrase often quoted in music: *prima le parole, e dopo la musica* (first the words, then the music). There are occasional examples in the 19th and 20th centuries of instrumental pieces with no words that are called "Songs without Words."

Opus
Latin for work, as in creative work.

Opera
The Italian singular for *opus* (work, creative work). The plural is opere. By extension (after 1600) *opera* came to mean a staged, sung dramatic work.

Movement
A distinct section of a piece of music.

Attacca (*attaccare* = to begin or start into)
Italian instruction placed at the end of a movement. In music, *attacca* means "to attack" or

jump right into the *next* movement with no pause.

Tempo
The speed of a piece of music. From the Latin noun for time (*tempus*)

Gramophone
The first working model was invented by Thomas Edison in 1877. Many inventors worldwide were interested in the idea. Edison's gramophone recorded sounds on tubular **waxed cylinders**, which could hold approximately 3 minutes of music. Another important inventor, Emile Berliner, perfected recording on flat discs similar to records. Ultimately, Berliner's format won out. Gramophones were acoustical, so in recording all sound went into a horn and was etched via a needle onto a surface. The playback reversed the process. The gramophone was powered, ultimately, by cranking a wind-up mechanism. There was, of course, no electricity and no electronic amplification.

Acoustics
The science of sound and hearing.

Register
Within any instrument or voice, the full scope (from high to low parts) of the notes that can be sounded. A piano has a large register (88 notes), while a human voice has a much smaller, or narrower, register.

Repertoire
The list or supply of musical works for a particular instrument, ensemble, or performer.

EXERCISES (in lieu of VIEWING GUIDE)

For Unit 1, there are four Listening Exercises (rather than a Viewing Guide). These now follow.

LISTENING EXERCISE 1
LEARNING TO LISTEN IN CONTEXT

In this exercise, you will get practice putting a "context" around the music you know and like. You will do this simply by *asking questions* about music that you ordinarily would simply listen to and enjoy.

1. Select *two* of your favorite songs or pieces of music. They can be any style or type of music. From now on, we will refer to these as "pieces" since not all pieces are songs ... but all songs are pieces!

2. Now, imagine you are leaving a description of each piece to be included in a time capsule. How would you describe this music to someone who had never heard it? What would you say?

3. After thinking about this, write a paragraph describing each piece: why you liked it, why it was (or wasn't!) really popular, etc. This will be tricky: you may be tempted just to toss in a recording for these future people to hear for themselves! But wait! If *you* were opening a time capsule from a century ago, there's a good chance that neither you, nor anyone you know, would have the ability to play a 78-RPM gramophone recording that was 100 years old. So, try to describe it in words.

Consider some of these points while writing your paragraph for each piece:

- What kinds of non-musical elements would help a future listener to appreciate the piece the way you do? (Say something about history, politics, pop culture, media.)

- What would the future listener need to know about contemporary life to appreciate this music: social situations, political events, types of worship, styles of dance, popular movies or television shows, etc?

- Is the piece you like generally popular, or just one of your favorites? Why or why not? What does that say about you as an individual?

- Where do you listen to this music? On what technology? Where is it designed to be heard? Describe those environments.

- What are you "supposed" to be doing while listening to this music? For instance, if you've selected an up-beat, pop dance tune, you might mention that many people like to listen to it while "working out." Be sure to explain to someone (a century now) what "working out" means! And what does the popularity of "working out" say about our culture?

Title and Artist, Piece No. 1 _____

Your Paragraph:

Title and Artist, Piece No. 2 _____

Your Paragraph:

LISTENING EXERCISE 2
I HEAR MUSIC: A LISTENING DIARY

Step 1. Choose two days in which to fill out the listening diary. Pick two days when you're likely to be out and about. If possible, pick two consecutive days. Add more "rows" to the charts if you need them.

Step 2. Estimate how many times you think you are likely to hear music during the selected day. Try to foresee the circumstances.

Step 3. Record every time you hear music of any kind. Use the sample chart below to get started. Either fill out the chart as the day goes on, or make notes and fill it out at the end of the day. Try to make the information as complete as possible. Make certain you record whether the "music" was heard voluntarily or involuntarily (if you prefer, use the terms passive and active).

Step 4. In essay or chart form, analyze what role music has played in each day's routine. How much of the "hearing" was voluntary and how much was involuntary? What was its effect on you or others? Was any of the music annoying or pleasing? Was there music you wouldn't have noticed had you not been conducting this survey?

SAMPLE CHART

NATURE OF MUSIC	WHEN/WHERE HEARD	METHOD OF DELIVERY	VOLUNTARY OR INVOLUNTARY	EFFECT ON YOU OR OTHERS?
1/3 of a pop song	Monday morning, through the wall of my sister's room before breakfast	Electronic: radio	Involuntary (passive)	Annoying
Some kind of fancy, quiet classical music	Monday, lunchtime, while I was on hold with T-Mobile trying to ask a question about my cell phone	Electronic: Cell phone	Involuntary (passive)	Kind of pretty at first, but then I was frustrated hearing it, because I waited so long.
Songs from High School Musical show	Monday afternoon, on school bus while we were coming back from our volleyball game	Live (I'm not sure I'd call it a performance, but it was fun!)	Voluntary (active)	Drove the bus driver crazy.

MY LISTENING DIARY, DAY 1: _____ (date)

I EXPECT TO HEAR MUSIC _____ TIMES TODAY

NATURE OF MUSIC	WHEN/WHERE HEARD	METHOD OF DELIVERY	VOLUNTARY OR INVOLUNTARY	EFFECT ON YOU OR OTHERS?

MY LISTENING DIARY, DAY 2: _____ **(date)**

I EXPECT TO HEAR MUSIC _____ TIMES TODAY

NATURE OF MUSIC	WHEN/WHERE HEARD	METHOD OF DELIVERY	VOLUNTARY OR INVOLUNTARY	EFFECT ON YOU OR OTHERS?

LISTENING EXERCISE 3
LISTENING ANALYTICALLY: NEW WAYS TO APPROACH SONGS

Directions: Choose three different songs or pieces. They can be familiar songs, or new, or some of each. They can be in any style: Country-Western, Show Music, Pop or Rock, Contemporary Christian, a song from a film, an older song of any style. Or, you can choose pieces from this course.

Make sure you have the whole piece available. A "clip" off the web or brief clip off of a soundtrack will not work as well, as you have no idea "where" you are in the piece.

Select one section from each piece to focus on: the opening, middle, or final section. This section should be between 1-2 minutes long. Listen repeatedly and carefully to each chosen section, focusing each time on one of the different musical qualities listed below.

You may answer in any order you like. However, you will probably find it easiest to observe these elements in the order given.

Warning! Do not stop at the first quick answer that pops into your head. Instead, be as detailed and descriptive as possible. You may find this is difficult to do at first, but be patient. Remember that developing listening is an art in and of itself that will serve you well in many different areas.

Tempo: How do you describe the tempo (speed) in this section? After your initial response ("fast" or "slow" isn't enough!), try the Italian terms (*allegro, andante, presto,* etc.) defined in Unit 3. Is the tempo steady, or does it change? Is the tempo an important factor shaping the way the piece sounds? In other words: would the piece have a different mood or affect if the tempo were very different?

Dynamics: What is the overriding dynamic level (volume) in this section? Loud (*forte*)? Soft (*piano*)? Somewhere in the middle (*mezzo piano/mezzo forte*)? Does the dynamic level change? Does the dynamic level help to shape the piece, or is the volume "simply there"?

Instrumentation: To the best of your ability to distinguish them, what instruments are playing in the section? If this is a vocal work (with a sung text), are the instruments simply part of a general background, supporting the vocal line, or does any one instrument specially interact with the vocal melody? To put it another way, does any instrument function as a solo instrument? *You may need to turn up the volume: professionally recorded music is often "mixed" to blend instruments together.*

Surface Rhythm: Describe the surface rhythm. Is the music characterized by quickly moving notes (fast surface rhythm), or are the notes longer, more sustained, and drawn out, with fewer notes passing by?

Texture: Texture is the "thickness" or "thinness" of the music. How many instruments or vocal melodies are going on? How busy is it "inside" of the music? In this section of the piece, how thick or thin is the texture?

Text: If the piece has words (lyrics), how much do the words influence the overall effect of the music? If the words were absent, would you still get the same feeling from this section of the music?

Harmonic Rhythm: To the best of your ability, analyze how quickly or slowly the chords or harmonies are changing. It may be easy to do this, depending on your experience with music and the simplicity of the piece(s) you have chosen. Or it may be challenging, and take repeated listening. Still, give it a try.

Piece No. 1 (name):

TEMPO

DYNAMICS

INSTRUMENTATION

SURFACE RHYTHM

TEXTURE

HARMONIC RHYTHM

TEXT

Piece No. 2 (name):

TEMPO
DYNAMICS
INSTRUMENTATION
SURFACE RHYTHM
TEXTURE
HARMONIC RHYTHM
TEXT

Piece No. 3 (name):

TEMPO
DYNAMICS
INSTRUMENTATION
SURFACE RHYTHM
TEXTURE
HARMONIC RHYTHM
TEXT

DISCUSSION QUESTION: When you've finished evaluating all three selections, write a short essay of three to four paragraphs describing the experience of listening specifically for *these* musical elements. How does this process differ from listening, in general, to music? Can you describe the differences? Does such listening add to, change, enhance, or (perhaps even) limit your appreciation of the piece?

LISTENING EXERCISE 4
ACROSS THE GENERATIONS: HEARING A SONG WITH NEW (OLD!) EARS

Step 1. Ask a person one or two generations older than you to suggest a favorite piece of music from his or her "youth" (teenage years or the years right out of high school).

Step 2. Get a recording of this music. You may be able to borrow it or use the services of your public library's music holdings, interlibrary loan (audio media usually can be ordered via interlibrary loan), or Internet resources such as iTunes or Amazon.

Step 3. Listen to the piece two or three times. Record your initial response as to the melody, rhythm, instrumentation, text, and overall expression on Part A of the form.

Step 4. Return to the person who suggested the piece to you. Ask some or all of the questions in Part B of the questionnaire.

Step 5. Compare the two responses—yours and the person for whom this music has special meaning.

Step 6. Write a 300-word essay explaining how your sense of the music changed when hearing about it via your recommender's memories.

If possible, share your essay with the person who recommended the song to you!

Worksheet

Song title: _____

Artist: _____

Year: _____

Part A. Your initial response

Tempo: 1   2   3   4   5   6   7
                           slow   medium   fast

Overall Energy: 1   2   3   4   5   6   7
                           relaxed   medium   energetic

Predominant dynamic range: soft / medium / loud

Vocal: one singer / duet / vocal group / instrumental only

Subject of text (if there is a text):

Predominant musical element(s)
- Particular instruments heard:
- Interesting harmonies:
- Strong percussion:
- Prominent melody:
- Distinctive rhythm:
- Memorable text:
- Particular atmosphere:

Good dance tune? yes   no

Good tune for listening, rather than for dancing? yes   no

Your overall reaction to the song:

Part B. Questions for the person who recommended the tune

Name of recommender:

Relationship to you (relative, friend, acquaintance, etc.):

When and where did you get to know this song/piece of music?

What were you doing at that time?

Did you know the artist(s) from another tune, or was this completely new to you?

Did you dance to this music?

Did you own a recording of this music? Do you still have it?

Did you keep your interest in the artist(s) and enjoy or even buy other music by him/her/them?

Did you ever see the performer(s) live in some kind of concert? If so, can you describe it?

Do you associate this music with someone or something specific in your life? A friend? A romantic interest? A family member? A favorite location or vacation spot?

Can you describe the memories this music brings back to you?

Do you have a funny or sentimental story or event associated with this music?

Why do you think you really liked this music back then?

When you listen to this music today, does it still strike you the same way?

Unit 1 Timeline

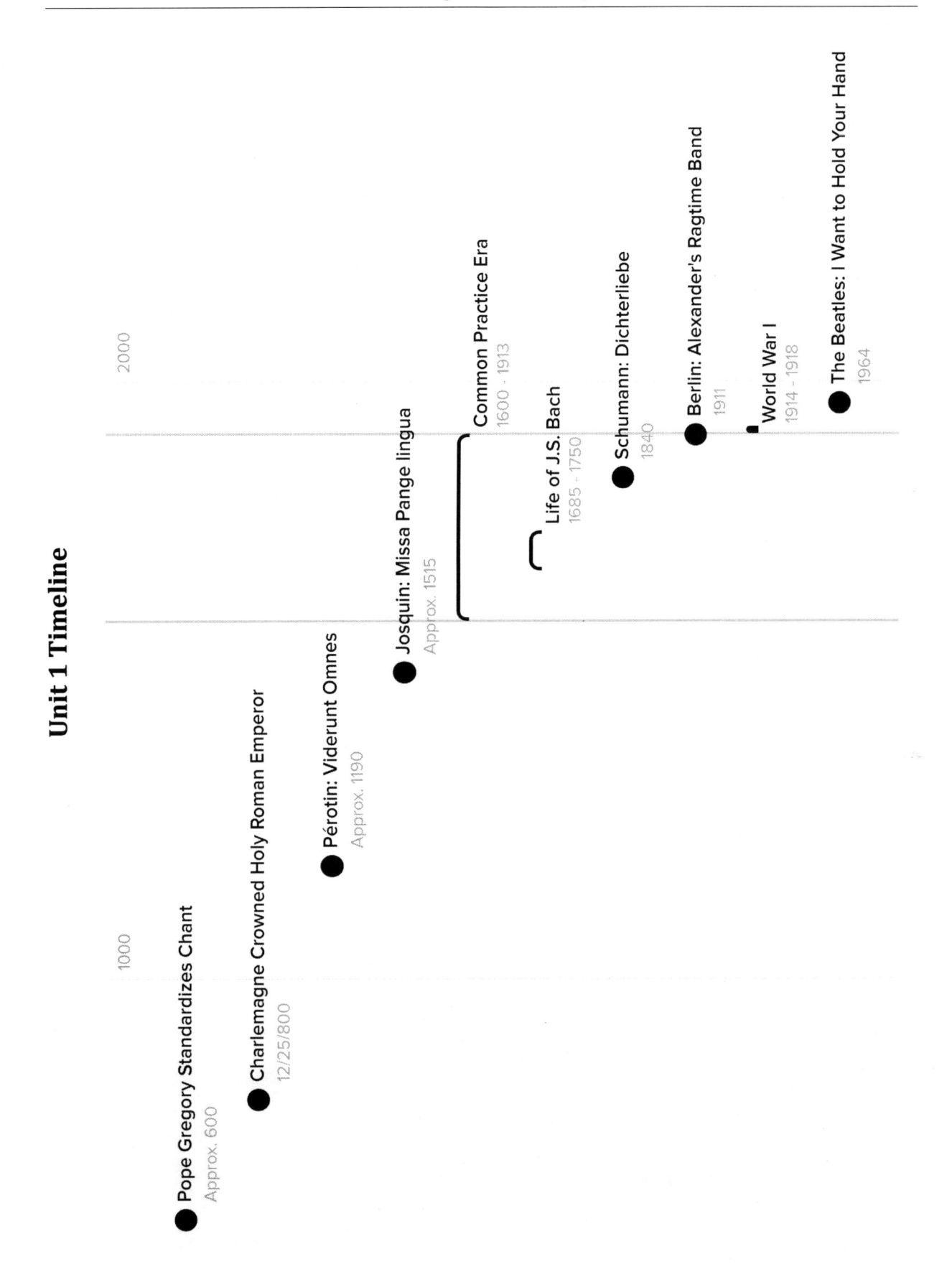

- **Pope Gregory Standardizes Chant** — Approx. 600
- **Charlemagne Crowned Holy Roman Emperor** — 12/25/800
- **Pérotin: Viderunt Omnes** — Approx. 1190
- **Josquin: Missa Pange lingua** — Approx. 1515
- **Common Practice Era** — 1600 - 1913
- **Life of J.S. Bach** — 1685 - 1750
- **Schumann: Dichterliebe** — 1840
- **Berlin: Alexander's Ragtime Band** — 1911
- **World War I** — 1914 - 1918
- **The Beatles: I Want to Hold Your Hand** — 1964

34 DISCOVERING MUSIC STUDENT WORKBOOK

YOUR TIMELINE

Dates ⟶

Unit 2

Music Entwined with Great Events in Western History

PEOPLE

Pythagoras
c. 570-490 BC
Ancient

Greece
Mathematician

Gregory I
the Great
c. 540-604
Medieval

Rome
Pope

Gutenberg
Johannes

c. 1400-1468
Renaissance

Germany
Inventor

Luther
Martin

1483-1546
Renaissance

Germany
Theologian

Galileo
Galileo Galilei

1551-1642
Renaissance

Italy
Astronomer, Physicist

Kepler
Johannes

1571-1630
Renaissance

Germany
Astronomer

Gabrieli
Giovanni

1554-1612
Renaissance/Baroque

Italy
Composer

Louis XIV
1638-1715
Baroque

France
King

PLACES

Eisenach, Germany (and Wartburg Castle)	50°57'58.83" N 10°18'22.83" E
Mainz, Germany	50°00'10.84" N 8°16'03.65" E
Wittenberg, Germany	51°52'00.00" N 12°38'41.64" E

VOCABULARY

Gregorian Chant
Also known as "plainsong" or "plainchant," this simple style of singing accounts for almost all surviving examples of written music from the early Medieval period. It was used in church for worship, and was sung without instrumental accompaniment (*a cappella*). This music was named "Gregorian" after Pope Gregory, who worked to standardize the chant throughout Europe (but did not actually write the tunes). "Chants" were traditionally sung in Latin and performed in the liturgy by monks or by the church's choir rather than the congregation.

Manuscript (*manus* = hand) + (*scriptum* = writing)
This Latin derivative describes the state and method of preserving information prior to the invention of Gutenberg's printing press. An entire category of people—mostly monks—were specifically trained as copyists to serve in *scriptoria*, special workspaces set aside for the painstaking work of copying *manuscripts*.

Notation
A general term to describe the system and process of writing down musical sounds, or notes. Initially, all notation was handwritten (in manuscript). Later musical notation was carved into intricate wooden blocks that could be inked (wood-block print). After the invention of the printing press, symbols for notes were set using tiny pieces of metal type (moveable type). Musical notation is more complicated to print than words because there are so many symbols.

Moveable Type
This method of printing enabled the printer to mix and match small pieces of type for text (both letters and numbers) to create words and sentences. As a result, printing became more flexible, faster, and less costly.

Engraving
Originally developed to meet the need for detailed, mass-produced images such as maps, engraving is the practice of carving any image into a soft metal plate. The carving, or scoring, of the plate must be done right-to-left, and "backwards" (as in a mirror-image). The plates are then inked and pressed onto parchment or paper. Engraving was especially helpful in printing images involving symbols or designs, such as maps, illustrations, or a musical score!

Lithography
Similar to engraving, except that images are etched into the plates by chemicals rather than scored by force into the metal. This resulted in a less expensive method of printing. Lithography was popular in the United States starting in the 19th century.

Reformation/Counter-Reformation
The Reformation is generally considered to have begun in 1517 by Martin Luther in an attempt to "reform" what he considered to be excesses in the Western Christian Church (Roman Catholic Church). The church ultimately responded with a series of ecumenical meetings called the Council of Trent (beginning in 1545) that had many purposes, including responding to the growing momentum of Luther's followers (Lutherans and other Protestant reformers). This was followed by a long period of Catholic revival popularly called the Counter-Reformation. Although these two movements initially centered around religious matters, the close relationship between the church and government in the 16th century meant that these conflicts became politicized.

Excommunication
The practice of withholding Communion (The Lord's Supper) to baptized church members who have not reconciled themselves to the Church's teaching, and purposefully have chosen to live in opposition to church doctrine.

Hymn
Although songs of praise were used as far back as Old Testament times, a new style of hymn became increasingly important in Lutheran and Protestant worship starting in the 16th century. These new hymns were perceived as simpler, more accessible than plainchant (Gregorian Chant). The tunes for these hymns were simple, often folk tunes, and each stanza of text reused the same tune. Also, while chants were typically sung in Latin, Protestant hymns were in the "vernacular"—the local language. Thus the Germans sang hymns in German, while the Dutch sang them in Dutch, etc.

Cantata
A dramatic work for voice(s) and instruments that conveys a story or theme. Cantatas were not staged or acted; rather, they had various purposes, including serving as vivid

musical illustrations of the theme of the worship service. The new Protestant churches in particular embraced the cantata for use in their services.

Gramophone
The gramophone was the earliest successful mechanical device invented to record and replay sound. Thomas Edison gets the credit for the invention (1877), although other inventors like Emile Berliner were working on similar devices in that same period. While envisioned as a device to record and preserve speech (and the voices of famous people), the gramophone became the new way to preserve and transmit music. In turn, it changed the dynamics of music-making forever because it gave the public access to music even when live performances were not available. Music no longer was constrained to real time (heard at the same time it was performed).

Tin Pan Alley
The space between West 28th Street and Fifth and Sixth Avenues in New York City, where dozens of music publishing houses were located as early as the 1880s. Hoping to convince a publisher to buy a song, songwriters would "pound out" tunes on pianos, either singing them or bringing a singer along to do so. If the song pleased, then it would be published. The sound of all these pianos flowed out the windows to create a cacophony best described as "the rattling of tin pans"—hence the name Tin Pan Alley.

Acoustics
The scientific study of sound and hearing. Sound is a quantifiable scientific property, governed by certain physical laws that can be studied, and even manipulated by outside forces to achieve a certain desired result.

DATES

1450	First printing press invented by German goldsmith Johannes Gutenberg in Mainz.
1517	On October 31, Martin Luther nailed his 95 Theses (objections against church practices) to a side door of the cathedral in the German town of Wittenberg, inadvertently beginning a reaction that resulted in the Protestant Reformation and, ultimately, the Thirty Years' War.
1545	Council of Trent. A series of meetings (Ecumenical Councils) held by the Catholic Church until 1563 whose purposes included clarifying doctrine and making reforms and to counter the growing appeal of the new Protestants. This was followed by a period of Catholic revival popularly known as the Counter-Reformation, generally dated between 1560 and the end of the Thirty Years' War, 1648.

1587	Sir Walter Raleigh's third expedition to North America sets out to establish a new colony at Roanoke (an island off the coast of North Carolina).
1607	Jamestown Settlement founded in what is now Virginia by the English "Virginia Company."
1618-1648	Thirty Years' War. A series of bloody religious conflicts to determine whether Europe would remain Catholic or become Protestant. Ultimately, little was solved, despite horrific death and damage. The northern part of Europe (today's Scandinavia, The Netherlands, Northern Germany) remained predominantly Protestant, while the southern part (today's Austria, Italy, Switzerland, Southern Germany) retained traditional Catholicism. Europeans as a whole still speak about the horror of this war, despite the centuries that have passed.
1620	Plymouth Colony, near Plymouth, Massachusetts, founded by the Pilgrims.
1666	A Royal Academy of Sciences is established by Louis XIV, showing his wholehearted support of modern (and often controversial) scientific research.
1682	William Penn founds Pennsylvania as a refuge for Quakers.
1929- 1939	The Great Depression, originating in the United States, but with parallels in Europe. Ultimately it is the preparation for, and execution of, World War II that brings an end to the economic hardships.

LISTENING

See Listening Guide at http://www.professorcarol.com/dm-listening

We consider a variety of works, again some outside the time frame of this course to gain a broader picture of music and history.

PUTTING IT ALL TOGETHER:

1. Regardless of your religion or religious affiliation, you should be aware of the tremendous role the Bible has played in the development of Western culture. Why do you think Gutenberg chose the Bible as his first major printing project? How was this Bible crucial to the development of the new industry of printing? Also, do a little research on the history of the English translation of the Bible.

2. Was the Council of Trent the first "council" to be held by the Roman Catholic Church? If not, why was it considered one of the most important? What was the *Index Liborum Prohibitorum*? What kinds of things were on it? What topics?

3. Do an online search on "Gutenberg." What is "Project Gutenberg"? Do you think Gutenberg would have approved? How might you or your family use this resource?

4. Luther's translation of the Bible into German was both a challenge to the authority of the Catholic Church and an important step in the standardization of the German language. How do you think this standardization contributed to the Thirty Years' War? What other impact did Luther's translation have on German culture?

5. Research the development of the radio. Try to determine how quickly radio went from an invention to an indispensable part of daily life. Seek statistics that document the economic impact of radio on the music industry and on advertising. Also, who were the first "stars" on the radio? Try, too, to find statistics indicating the present status of radio within the entertainment industry.

6. Look up the Renaissance instruments Cornetto and Sackbut. What are their modern equivalents and how do they differ both in terms of how they sound and how they are played? What other Renaissance instruments can you discover? Find several performances online (preferably with video)

7. Generally esteemed as the originator of mathematical ideas, Pythagoras (c. 570-c. 490 BC) is heralded for his accomplishments in music too. See what you can learn about his contributions to the science we call of acoustics and to music theory. Explore the debate as to whether it was actually Pythagoras, or his students, or other figures, who made these discoveries.

8. The development of the gramophone changed culture. It was more than a new technology, affecting how people listened to music, studied and performed music, as well as social dynamics like dance and fashion. It spawned a new industry worldwide—the recording industry. Research this topic, and develop one of the following 1) an outline of the gramophone's invention, growth, and impact, 2) a set of questions and answers about this phenomenon, or 3) a profile of several of the earliest recording artists, including what kind of things they recorded (note: some of these early recordings contained speeches and poetry).

Unit 2: Music Entwined with Great Events in Western History 41

VIEWING GUIDE

1. The rise of radio in the _____ (decade) changed the popular music industry because _____ _____. The Internet has caused another set of changes, particularly because _____ _____.

2. One of the most important technological innovations in Western history came with the invention of the _____ in _____ (place) by _____ (person). Books were printed on both _____ _____ and _____.

3. The _____ (which country?) actually first used the idea of printing with moveable type (both ceramic and wood).

4. Before the invention of the printing press, how were "books" produced? _____ _____ _____.

5. Parchment is actually made of _____! Gutenberg used both parchment and paper: about _____ sheep were needed for each of the 35 parchment copies of Gutenberg's Bible.

6. Scholars estimate that, prior to Gutenberg, there were about _____ hand-copied books in Europe. Within fifty years, more than _____ books were circulating.

7. How was music reproduced in the Medieval period? _____ _____.

8. Did anything in the earliest musical notation indicate whether the notes were long or short in duration (length)? Yes   No

9. During the 16th century, printers started to use the process of engraving, which was already well developed by _____ (what profession?).

10. The difficult thing about engraving is that every image must be etched (how?) _____.

11. _____, called "the poor man's engraving," was done not by etching, but with the use of chemicals.

12. How did the gramophone affect popular music, including the sale of printed music? _____
_____
_____.

13. In what American city do you find Tin Pan Alley? _____ What commercial activity went on there? _____
_____

14. How did Tin Pan Alley get its name? _____
_____
_____.

15. Using the science of _____, we can analyze and explain every sound in the universe.

16. Modern acoustical understanding was based on the work of early Greek mathematician _____.

17. Architecture and acoustics have been intertwined for centuries, for example _____
_____.

18. _____ (nationality) King Louis XIV was a powerful European monarch. A modern thinker, he used the _____ as his symbol, connecting him to _____.

19. Scientists examining the relationship of the planets and sun during this era included _____ and _____.

20. The age known as _____ was characterized by scientific achievement and the collecting of knowledge. Artists and thinkers in the following century were more concerned with _____
_____
_____.

Unit 2 Timeline

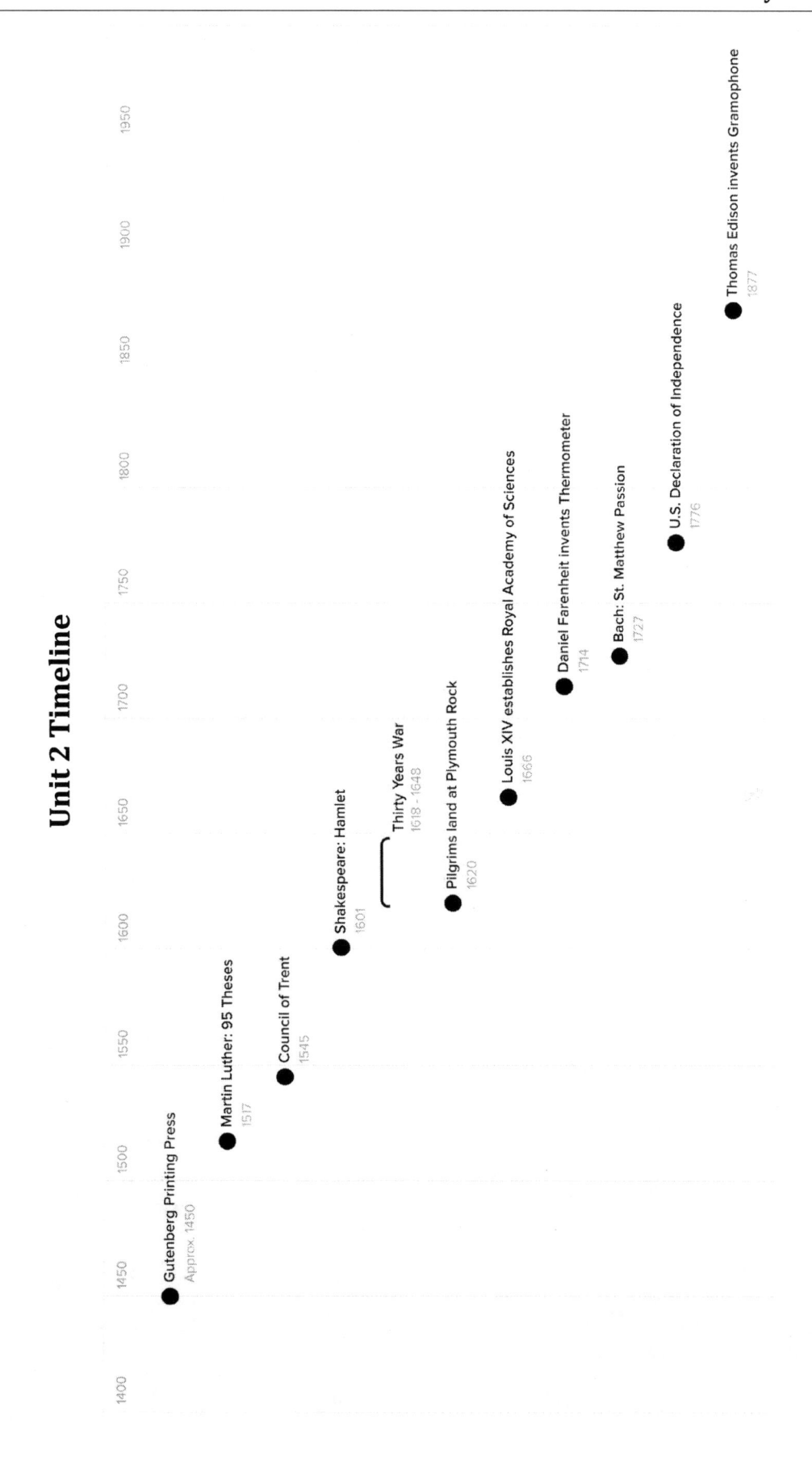

Approx. 1450	Gutenberg Printing Press
1517	Martin Luther: 95 Theses
1545	Council of Trent
1601	Shakespeare: Hamlet
1618–1648	Thirty Years War
1620	Pilgrims land at Plymouth Rock
1666	Louis XIV establishes Royal Academy of Sciences
1714	Daniel Farenheit invents Thermometer
1727	Bach: St. Matthew Passion
1776	U.S. Declaration of Independence
1877	Thomas Edison invents Gramophone

YOUR TIMELINE

Dates →

Unit 3

Technology, Terminology, and Cultural Perspective

VOCABULARY

Genre
From the Latin genus, for birth, family, or nation. In music, genre means the type, kind, or category of music, referring to its function and form. Genres include symphony, string quartet, opera, oratorio, cantata, ballet, tone poem, character piece, and dance.

Symphony
A piece of music written for a large group of instruments (usually an orchestra). It is generally divided into multiple, distinct sections called *movements*. Remember: an orchestra is the group that plays the music. A symphony is a genre or type of music. You will find orchestras with the word "symphony" in their title, such as the London Symphony Orchestra or the Chicago Symphony Orchestra.

Quartet
A genre of music played by four players, usually strings (two violins, one viola, and one cello), but any combination of four players (or singers) makes up a quartet.

Opera
A story presented by singers on a stage. Performances involve singing, acting, costumes, lights, and staging. Thus, operas are referred to as being "staged" or dramatic works.

Concerto
From the Italian verb concertare, meaning to agree or to harmonize. Music for this genre usually involves a soloist (sometimes a small group acting as a "soloist" together) playing in some kind of musical conversation with a larger group.

Movements
The divisions of a musical composition. Movements usually have a distinct beginning and ending (sometimes making them seem like separate, individual pieces). Here's an analogy: a book (like a composition) consists of separate chapters (or movements). Each chapter can have subdivisions (or sections).

Virtuoso (plural Virtuosi or Virtuosos)
An extraordinarily gifted or capable performer. The incredibly difficult music that virtuosi play is referred to as "virtuosic," and often has been composed simply to show off the performer's exceptional ability, or virtuosity.

Tempo
Literally, this word is Italian for "time." This term is used to refer to the speed of music. You can describe *tempo* with the following terms (all are Italian):

Presto, or "quick"

Vivo, or "lively," from the Latin verb *vivere* (to live)

Andante, literally, at a "walking pace" from the verb *andare* (to go). Be careful! Sometimes this term is perceived as "slow." But think of all the different speeds people use to "go": if you have a little brother or sister, you know how fast (or slow) "go" can be! Conventions of style sometimes help musicians know how fast "andante" should be in a given piece.

Allegro, "cheerful," "merry," "happy," or "lively" and, thus, a moderately quick tempo

Adagio, or "at ease" or "at leisure," and, thus, a slow tempo (slower than Andante)

Largo, or "broadly" and, thus, a slow tempo (slower than Andante)

Molto/Meno
Italian for "much" and "less." These are "flavoring" words, which can be added as adverbs to other terms.

Ensemble
From the Latin root *insimul*, meaning "simultaneous" or "at the same time." A group of instruments or singers making music together.

LISTENING

See Listening Guide at http://www.professorcarol.com/dm-listening

We continue to consider works outside the timeframe of this course as we build a better understanding of instruments and the elements of music.

PUTTING IT ALL TOGETHER

1. Carefully study and memorize the terms for tempo (speed) in this unit. Think of a specific thing or activity that each Italian term for tempo represents to you; you could even find a picture for each in a newspaper, magazine, or online. Search for one or more pieces of music that expresses your sense of each term.

2. Get acquainted with the main types and sizes of musical ensembles in Western classical music:

Be able to answer the following questions:

- What are vocal ensembles called?
- Are there any ensembles in which instruments and voices are mixed?
- What is the difference between an "orchestra" and a "string orchestra"?
- What is the difference between an "orchestra" and a "chamber orchestra"?
- What are the families of instruments within the orchestra?
- Which instruments belong to which families?

3. If you are unfamiliar with the instruments used in Western bands and orchestras (violins, oboes, trumpets, bassoons, trumpets, tubas, timpani, etc.), spend some time in this unit becoming acquainted with them. You can find much material by searching in your local library or online.

4. Find out the cost that goes into the purchase of musical instruments. What family of instruments, in general, is the most costly? Why? How (and where) are instruments made? What family of instruments will last for the longest number of years? The shortest? Do instruments keep their value?

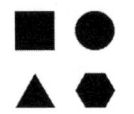

5. Looking online, find one of the following pieces that shows the video performance: a piano concerto by Beethoven; a symphony by Haydn, Mozart, or Beethoven; a string quartet by Haydn, Mozart, or Beethoven. Select any movement (the first movement may be easiest to work with). Listen to three different performances by different musicians. Consider looking for a contrast between seasoned performers (older musicians) and younger players (college or even high school). After listening to the contrasting performances, write or discuss your impressions and the effect the different recordings had. Would these impressions have been the same, do you think, if you had encountered your chosen performances in a different order?

VIEWING GUIDE

1. Talking about form really means discussing the _____ of something.

2. Form is all around us, and easy to see in things like (examples) _____ _____ _____.

3. "Movements" are _____.

4. Where are tempo markings usually located on the page of a musical score? _____.

5. *Allegro* means _____.

6. *Andante* means _____.

7. *Adagio* and *largo* have similar (but not identical) meanings. *Adagio* means _____, and *largo* means _____.

8. *Presto* means _____, and *vivo* comes from the Latin verb _____, and means "quickly."

9. _____ and _____ mean "less" and "much" (very).

10. Did composers always indicate tempo markings? _____. Justify your answer. _____ _____.

11. We can compare the talents and skills of a virtuoso performer to _____ _____.

12. Understanding _____ is the key to music-making.

13. *Genre* means a _____.

14. Giving specific names to genres and styles can get confusing because _____ _____ _____.

15. A symphony is usually written for a _____ (size) group of instruments.

16. Is a quartet always played by stringed instruments like violins, violas, and cellos? _____

17. The basic idea of opera goes back to the _____.

18. "Concerto" comes from the Italian verb *concertare*, which means _____.

19. How large is an ensemble? Does it have a set size? Has it been the same size throughout music history? (explain) _____

50 DISCOVERING MUSIC STUDENT WORKBOOK

YOUR TIMELINE

Dates ⟶

Unit 4

Fanfare and Power: The Court of Louis XIV

PEOPLE

Louis XIV
1638-1715
Baroque

France
King

Lully
Jean-Baptiste
1632-1687
Baroque

France
Composer

Harvey
William
1578-1657
Baroque

England
Physician

Le Brun
Charles
1619-1690
Baroque

France
Artist

Molière
Jean-Baptiste Poquelin
1622-1673
Baroque

France
Playwright

Charpentier
Marc-Antoine
1643-1704
Baroque

France
Composer

Couperin
Louis

1626-1661
Baroque

France
Composer

Couperin
François

1668-1733
Baroque

France
Composer

Froberger
Johann Jacob

1616-1667
Baroque

France
Composer

Mouret
Jean-Joseph

1682-1738
Baroque

France
Composer

PLACES

| Paris, France | 48°51'23.81" N 2°21'08.00" E |
| Versailles, France | 48°48'17.51" N 2°07'13.28" E |

VOCABULARY

Versailles
Originally a hunting château, Versailles was built into Europe's greatest royal palace. Nearly every other European monarchy modeled its palaces after Versailles, borrowing its architecture, landscaping, and fountains as the ultimate model of imperial power demonstrated by human design.

Court
This general word can actually apply to a number of things. The "court" can refer to a physical location, as in being "at court." It can also refer to the group of people who were gathered around a monarch, as in being a "member of the court" of Louis XIV.

Château
In French, literally, "house"; a term usually referring to great houses built in the country. Though not intended to be palaces, these houses had to be large enough for the noble family, visitors, and the domestic employees. As a result, they can be as large (and grand) as a palace.

Fête
In French: party, festival, or birthday. This word is used to indicate celebrations; if you wish someone "Happy Birthday" in French, you will say, "*Bonne fête.*"

Divertissement
In French, literally, a diversion or light entertainment. A *divertissement* is usually a short musical piece, often for dancing, that was intended to be an interlude during breaks in a larger, longer, often more serious performance. These sometimes functioned as an intermission feature.

Faux pas
In French, literally, "false step." A false step during the court dance.

Dauphin
The title given to the son of a French monarch (usually the oldest son) who was the intended heir to the throne. Although we usually think of such an individual as a "prince," many monarchies (and many languages) use a specific term to refer to the next king, separating him from the other "ordinary" princes.

Salle
In French, a large hall or auditorium. The Hall of Mirrors is called *Salle des glaces*. Compare *glaces* with glaze and glass.

Maître de musique
French for "master of music," usually an official title conferred by a king to one composer in a supervisory position.

Overture
A composition for instruments only. It serves as an introduction to a longer work such as the opening for a ballet or opera. It comes from the French verb *ouvrir*, to open. Usually, an overture is very catchy and fun to listen to, sometimes offering shortened versions of the melodies to follow. Overtures originally had a practical purpose: before it became customary in the late 19th century to lower the house lights, an overture alerted the audience that the performance was about to begin.

Männerchor (*Männer* = men) + (*Chor* = choir)
In German, a choir of male singers. It is a long-standing tradition in German folk music. Even today, small villages will boast a very proficient men's choir.

Kapellmeister (*Kapelle* = Chapel) + (*Meister* = master)

In German, the "master of the chapel," who was responsible for composing and/or directing musical performances in the chapel and, by extension, the entire court. The French equivalent is *maître de chapelle*.

Fasching

In German, this is another word for Carnival, the unofficial season of feasting and parties that leads up to Lent. You will also find the spelling *Carnaval* and *Carnevale*.

Les Vingt-quatre Violons du Roi

In French, "The twenty-four violins of the King," a carefully trained string ensemble conducted by Lully during his service to Louis XIV.

DATES

1610	Santa Fe established as the capital of New Mexico.
1630-1643	English Puritans immigrate to the Massachusetts Bay colony.
1661	Coronation of Louis XIV. He establishes Versailles as the official residence in 1682.
1664	New Amsterdam becomes "New York."
1670	Hudson's Bay Company chartered.

LISTENING

See Listening Guide at http://www.professorcarol.com/dm-listening

Selections for this Unit focus on music that would have accompanied events at the court of Versailles.

PUTTING IT ALL TOGETHER

1. Research the history of Versailles' famous Hall of Mirrors. Pay special attention to the events taking place there in 1871 and in 1919. In what condition did the hall (and Versailles in general) survive World War II? Were there other significant political events there in the twentieth century? Has the hall been renovated recently? How long did this take?

2. Consider any special music performance spaces in your neighborhood or city. How many are there? Are they used for music only? If not, what other kinds of performances are scheduled? How are they different from Versailles, and why? Many performance venues today are called "Performing Arts centers" and may be very large buildings that house a number of different spaces. If you have access to one of these, try to arrange a field trip. If that is not possible, look at the schedule of productions for a period of time and draw some conclusions about the performances offered and the intended audiences.

3. One of the music performance spaces in your neighborhood is probably your church or house of worship. Even if the music there is performed only as part of worship services, this may be a place where you frequently hear live music. Spend some time interviewing your *Kapellmeister* or music director (music minister). Explain that you have been thinking more about live musical performances. Tell him or her that you are interested in knowing what kind of decisions and activities take place "behind the scenes," since that person's job is to provide live music on a weekly basis. Some questions you might ask include:

- How did you get this job, and how long have you had it?

- What kind of preparation is required for this sort of job, including education or prior experience?

- What are the most important things that you consider when planning services? How long does this typically take?

- Are there other, non-service, musical performances? Are there rules or policies for these?

- What do you like most about your performance space? What would you like to change?

- Are there others (audio engineers, video engineers, etc.) who are involved in making the music happen?

- How much rehearsal or practice time occurs each week?

- Are extra or guest musicians ever hired?

- What are some extra things that you would like, but cannot fit into the budget? Why would they be helpful?

4. Spend some time researching America's National Endowment for the Arts. When was it founded, and by whom? What are the stated purposes of the organization? What are some examples of its most recent projects? Consider carefully the advantages and disadvantages of state-sponsored art: what were some of the pitfalls of "government" (royal) funding for the arts during Louis' day? Do these same challenges still exist, or have modern times brought different, modern problems?

5. Although Versailles was built long ago, it has retained its status. The palace is one of the world's top tourist destinations. What can you find out about Versailles role in French culture and economy today? What is involved in visiting? How much does it cost and what allotment of time would you need? Are there ever concerts, events, and conferences held within the palace?

6. Examine the history of music in the White House. See if you can find artists who have played for presidents and their guests in the White House. Try to find other cultural events that take place in the White House and on its grounds. Do you find support for the statement that the artistic events scheduled there reflect each particular president's personal interests?

7. Compare the painting of Versailles by Pierre Patel in 1668 (see Text for this Unit) with contemporary photographs of the palace, especially any aerial photographs you can find. How has the palace changed since Louis XIV's time? Learn what you can about the layout and life of the town of Versailles today.

Unit 4: Fanfare and Power: The Court of Louis XIV

VIEWING GUIDE

1. Three major institutions that have supported art throughout Western Culture: _____, _____, and _____.

2. What are the differences between voluntary and involuntary listening experiences? _____ _____.

3. For much of Western music history, why were most choirs for boys only? _____ _____.

4. European monarchs used the palace of _____ as their model for power and extravagance both during Louis XIV's lifetime and for centuries afterwards.

5. A _____ is the head of all of the church music and may also be in charge of an entire court musical establishment.

6. The _____ was the keyboard instrument of choice in those days, and it fit well with the aristocracy.

7. In terms of power, we call the 17th and 18th centuries the Age of _____ _____. Powerful monarchs included _____ _____.

8. Although it is huge, Louis XIV's palace of Versailles is called a _____, which means "house." It was built originally to be a _____.

9. During the Age of Absolutism, monarchs would do almost anything to acquire the best _____. Why? Because the arts were a symbol of power!

10. Louis XIV was known as the _____ (nickname), which associated him with _____.

11. Paintings of Alexander the Great brought attention to a painter named _____ who would become Court Painter.

12. During this time, scientists were developing a modern understanding of the _____. One of the ways Louis XIV demonstrated his support of the new sciences was to _____

58 DISCOVERING MUSIC STUDENT WORKBOOK

_____.

13. Louis XIV was a great _____. His courtiers were expected to join in. In his court, a mistaken step, known as a _____, could cause a demotion in a career. As Louis XIV grew older, the dancing masters at court needed to be diplomatic and make sure _____ _____, who no longer could execute the most difficult steps.

14. Louis XIV also had a great impact on fashion and on technology. His elegant taste is best seen in a grand room called _____ ___. This room was also the site for important events in more recent history, including _____ _____.

15. The composer Lully teamed up with the great playwright of the era named _____ for some fantastic productions.

16. Music accompanied everything King Louis XIV did, including _____ _____.

17. A popular type of music called a _____ is particularly fitting for this period, especially with the grand opening chords and dotted rhythms (long, short-long, short-long).

18. When you go to visit _____, you'd better set aside at least three days: one for the _____ and two for the _____.

Unit 4 Timeline

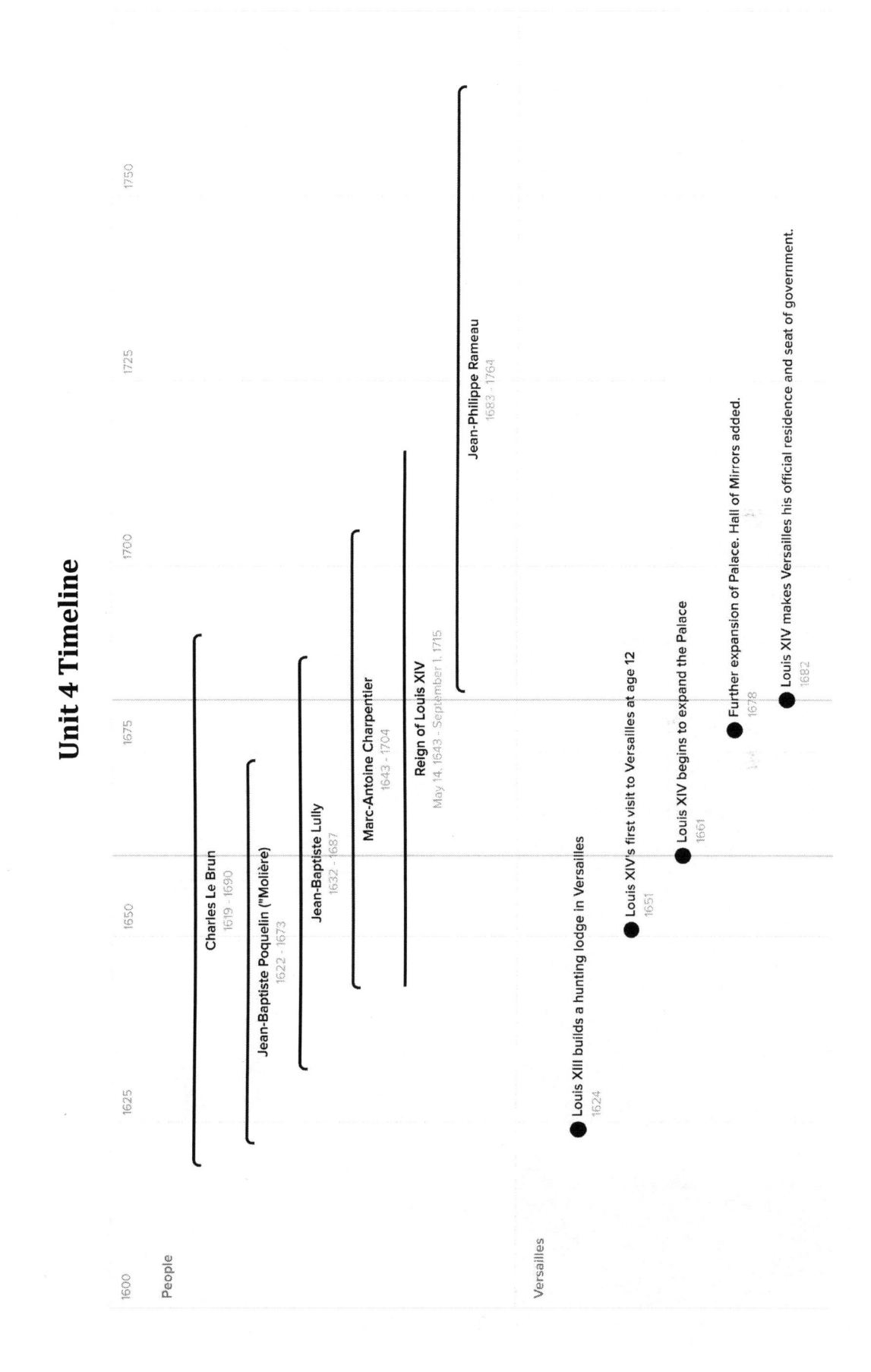

People

- Charles Le Brun — 1619 - 1690
- Jean-Baptiste Poquelin ("Molière") — 1622 - 1673
- Jean-Baptiste Lully — 1632 - 1687
- Marc-Antoine Charpentier — 1643 - 1704
- Reign of Louis XIV — May 14, 1643 - September 1, 1715
- Jean-Philippe Rameau — 1683 - 1764

Versailles

- 1624 — Louis XIII builds a hunting lodge in Versailles
- 1651 — Louis XIV's first visit to Versailles at age 12
- 1661 — Louis XIV begins to expand the Palace
- 1678 — Further expansion of Palace. Hall of Mirrors added.
- 1682 — Louis XIV makes Versailles his official residence and seat of government.

Unit 4: Fanfare and Power: The Court of Louis XIV

YOUR TIMELINE

Dates ⟶

Unit 5

Sweeping Away the Renaissance into the Baroque

PEOPLE

Dante
Dante Aligheri

c. 1265-1321
Medieval

Italy
Writer

Boccaccio
Giovanni

1313-1375
Renaissance

Italy
Writer

Brunelleschi
Filippo

1377-1446
Renaissance

Italy
Architect

Luther
Martin

1483-1546
Renaissance

Germany
Theologian

Leonardo
Leonardo da Vinci

1452-1519
Renaissance

Italy
Artist, Architect

Newton
Isaac

1643-1727
Baroque

England
Physicist

Hus
Jan

1372-1415
Renaissance

Bohemian
Theologian

Byrd
William

c. 1539-1623
Renaissance

English
Composer

Tallis
Thomas

c. 1505-1585
Renaissance

England
Composer

Dowland
John

1563-1626
Renaissance

England
Composer

PLACES

| Florence, Italy | 43°46'23.53" N 11°15'19.36" E |
| Venice, Italy | 45°26'02.80" N 12°20'20.47" E |

VOCABULARY

Renaissance
Literally, "re-birth." This term refers to the rebirth of ideas from Classical (Ancient) Greece and Rome within European culture starting in the mid-14th century.

Recitative
A style of singing used when much dialogue or informative text must be related. The text is in prose and is essentially "recited" to music, using a free rhythm and style that resembles speech.

Aria
In contrast to recitative, an aria (or "air") is the lyrical portion of an opera, the song-like sections where emotions are expressed using melody. Aria texts usually are poetic

(rhyming) and the music has a definite beat (metrical).

Monody
A musical style or texture featuring a single line of melody.

Prima/Seconda Prattica
A lively debate among composers of Monteverdi's time centered around these two "practices." The "first practice" (*Prima Prattica*), characteristic of pre-Baroque music, emphasized the older and more elaborate (polyphonic) style of composition. The "second practice" (*Seconda Prattica*), in direct contrast, focused on a simplified style called monody that highlighted a single melody.

Opera
Literally, "work," in Italian. Later, it came to mean a genre featuring a story that is set to music and "staged" with costumes, sets, acting, and even dance.

Toccata
From the Italian *toccare*, meaning "to touch." Composed for keyboard instruments or stringed instruments like the lute, this type of instrumental piece was designed to highlight the performer's technical ability—literally, how well the player could "touch" the instrument!

Libretto (plural *Libretti*, Librettos)
The "little book" (from *libro*) that provides the script for an opera or oratorio. The text was printed in small format (hence libretto) and sold cheaply to audience members. The libretto shapes the work (remember: *Prima le parole, e dopo la musica*). Throughout much of Western music history, the individual writing the libretto (*librettist*) had greater status than the composer.

Lieto Fine
"Happy ending." Even tragic works during the Baroque period required a *lieto fine*.

Polyphony (*poly* = many) + (*phon* =sound)
This style, or texture, of music features many melodies (each independent) interwoven into one complex musical fabric.

Counterpoint
A musical texture in which independent melodic lines (instrumental or vocal) interweave according to a strict set of rules based on the mathematical relationship of the simultaneous sounds.

Consonance/Dissonance
Two contrasting words for describing the basic quality of music. Music that is "consonant" features sounds that are pleasing, and fit together well. "Dissonant" music is most quickly recognized as clashing combinations of sounds that create tension and a general sense of unrest.

Basso Continuo

Also known as "figured bass," *basso continuo* was a common musical texture in the Baroque era. It requires two parts: an instrument that plays chords or harmonies, such as a keyboard or lute, and a low instrument with sustained sound such as a bassoon or cello able to produce a bass line as a foundation.

Fantasia

A certain kind of instrumental work that was intended to sound "fantastic" or inventive. Loosely organized in several sections, a fantasia would go from fast to slow, loud to soft, simple to complex, allowing the performer to show off all styles of playing. A *fantasia* could also have highly structured sections (counterpoint).

Fugue

A very intricate form of polyphony, in which there are a specific number of musical lines or voices (usually four) that all present and develop the same musical idea. A fugue is the most sophisticated type of counterpoint, or contrapuntal composition.

Tragedie lyrique

In French, literally "lyrical tragedy." This was a French style of courtly operatic drama, somewhat similar to Italian *opera seria*.

LISTENING

See Listening Guide at http://www.professorcarol.com/dm-listening

As we move from the Renaissance to the Baroque with Monteverdi's opera *Orfeo*, let us also consider examples of the new Protestant music and two Elizabethan composers: Thomas Tallis and John Dowland.

PUTTING IT ALL TOGETHER

1. Someone who is well educated and has many different abilities and interests is sometimes known as a "Renaissance Man." Study the life and works of Leonardo da Vinci and consider whether he was a true "Renaissance Man." The following questions may help you to craft your findings:

What kind of education did da Vinci receive?

What were some of his major discoveries?

What were some of da Vinci's greatest artistic works?

What scientific experiments did he conduct?

2. Construct a concise essay that serves to introduce the works of of Boccaccio and Dante? What were their most significant writings? How would you explain, briefly, their importance to Italian and Western culture? Also, what historical tragedy occurred to influence Boccaccio's career as a writer?

3. Study the images of Brunelleschi's dome at the cathedral in Florence (*Duomo di Firenze*). Why was it so remarkable when it was built? Then study images of St. Mark's Basilica in Venice. How are these two spaces alike? How are they different? Which one is older? What influence did these two domes have on subsequent architecture?

4. Explore the history of Florence, Italy. What has made it one of the most remarkable cities of the world? What artistic events would the city offer to you if you could spend a substantial amount of time in Florence?

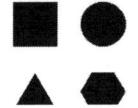

5. Look for a website or other resource on Baroque musical instruments. How do these instruments differ from their modern versions? Is there a difference between how certain instruments, such as a violin or cello, was played in Baroque time and now? Find (online) a principal Baroque work that is performed using Baroque, or original, instruments and compare that performance with one played by the modern orchestra. Works that should make this easy include any of Bach's Brandenburg Concerti, Handel's *Water Music* or *Music for the Royal Fireworks*, or Vivaldi's *The Seasons*.

6. The years from 1550 to 1700 spanned an incredible period of scientific development. Many modern discoveries were made, based upon the study of chemistry, zoology, botany, pharmacology, natural sciences, and the human body. Spend some time researching the lives and works of Newton and Leibniz. Who were their contemporaries? How were they educated? What were some of their most important discoveries?

66 DISCOVERING MUSIC STUDENT WORKBOOK

VIEWING GUIDE

1. We use the term _____ to describe the approximately three hundred years from 1600 to 1900 when music _____ _____ _____.

2. There are six common qualities of music during the Common Practice Era, including (provide 3) _____ _____ _____.

3. The city of _____ was a perfect city for artistic experimentation during the Renaissance. Famous residents included _____ _____.

4. The most significant new genre of the Common Practice Era, invented in Florence, had various names at first, but eventually would be called _____.

5. The term "Renaissance" means _____.

6. Increased focus on human achievement is usually called _____.

7. The career of Italian composer _____ spanned the late Renaissance into the Baroque Era. His musical style changed from _____ _____ to _____.

8. The 1607 opera *Orfeo* was called a _____.

9. Opera is essentially a _____ where all (or part) of the script is _____.

10. Instrumentation means _____.

11. What architectural structure inspired Gabrieli's compositions? _____ _____.

12. In Greek mythology, who was Orpheus? _____ _____.

13. A _____ is a theatrical requirement for ending a Baroque drama.

14. Many of the stories upon which Baroque operas (and even some

Unit 5: Sweeping Away the Renaissance into the Baroque   67

modern operas) are based can be traced back to _____ _____.

15. "Baroque" is a French word for the Portuguese *barrôco* which meant _____. Initially the term (circle one) was / was not positive in meaning.

16. Monophony means _____. Throughout the Medieval period, music became more _____.

17. Writing down music by hand in what we call _____ was actually a high-tech skill.

18. *Basso continuo* is created by how many players, playing what kinds of instruments? _____ _____.

19. Two popular Baroque genres of pieces for keyboard, lute, or guitar were the _____ (from the Italian verb "to touch") and the _____.

20. A fugue is a _____ _____.

21. *Recitative* conveys primarily _____, while an aria is _____.

22. Serious Baroque opera based on mythology became known as _____ _____. In the early 18th century, short, comic episodes called _____ were placed between the acts of these serious works.

23. Throughout the Baroque era, who could afford to sponsor operatic productions? _____

24. The word _____ means "work" in Latin. Later the Italian form, _____, came to describe the whole genre of staged, sung works.

Unit 5 Timeline

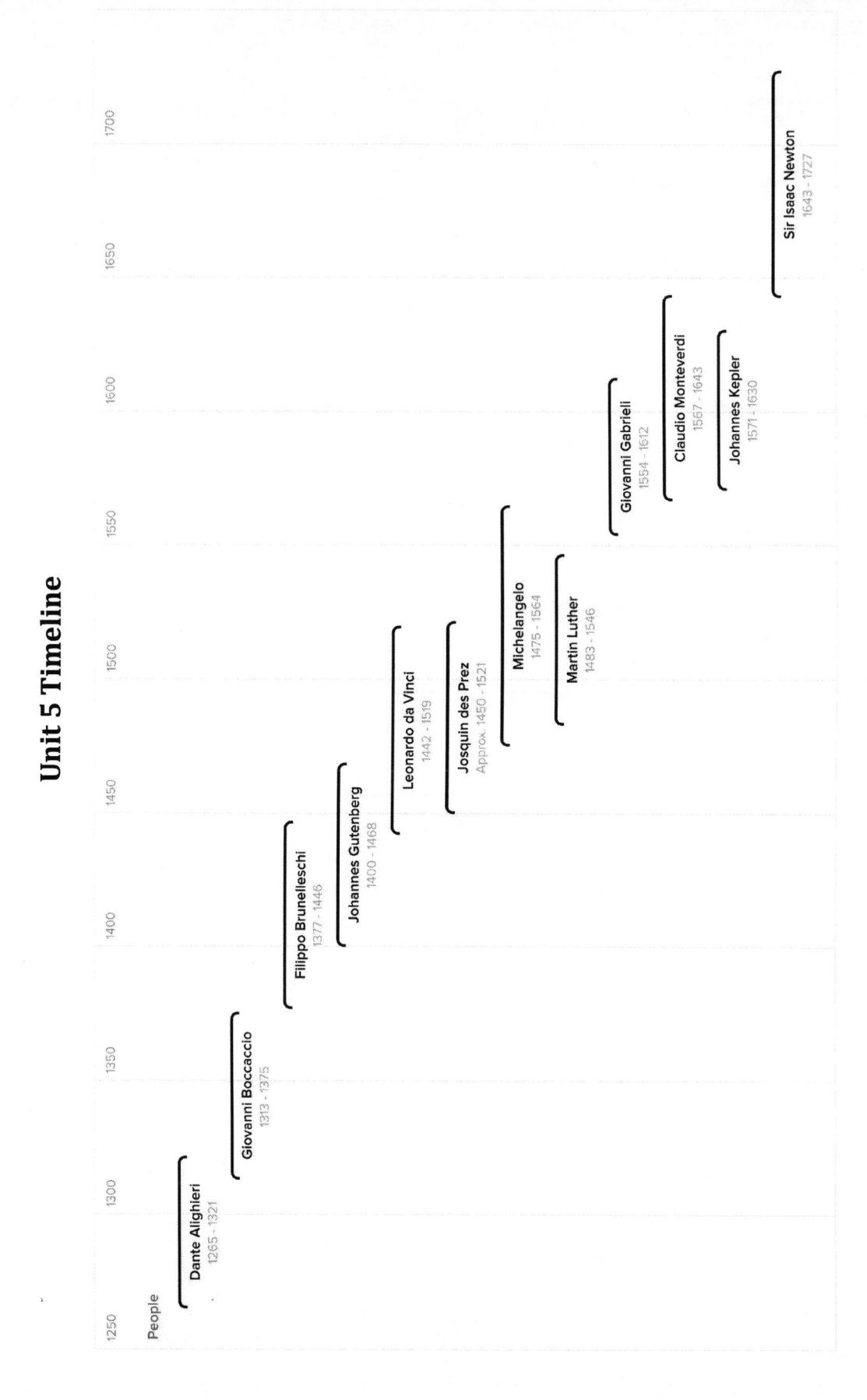

People

- Dante Alighieri, 1265 - 1321
- Giovanni Boccaccio, 1313 - 1375
- Filippo Brunelleschi, 1377 - 1446
- Johannes Gutenberg, 1400 - 1468
- Leonardo da Vinci, 1442 - 1519
- Josquin des Prez, Approx. 1450 - 1521
- Michelangelo, 1475 - 1564
- Martin Luther, 1483 - 1546
- Giovanni Gabrieli, 1554 - 1612
- Claudio Monteverdi, 1567 - 1643
- Johannes Kepler, 1571 - 1630
- Sir Isaac Newton, 1643 - 1727

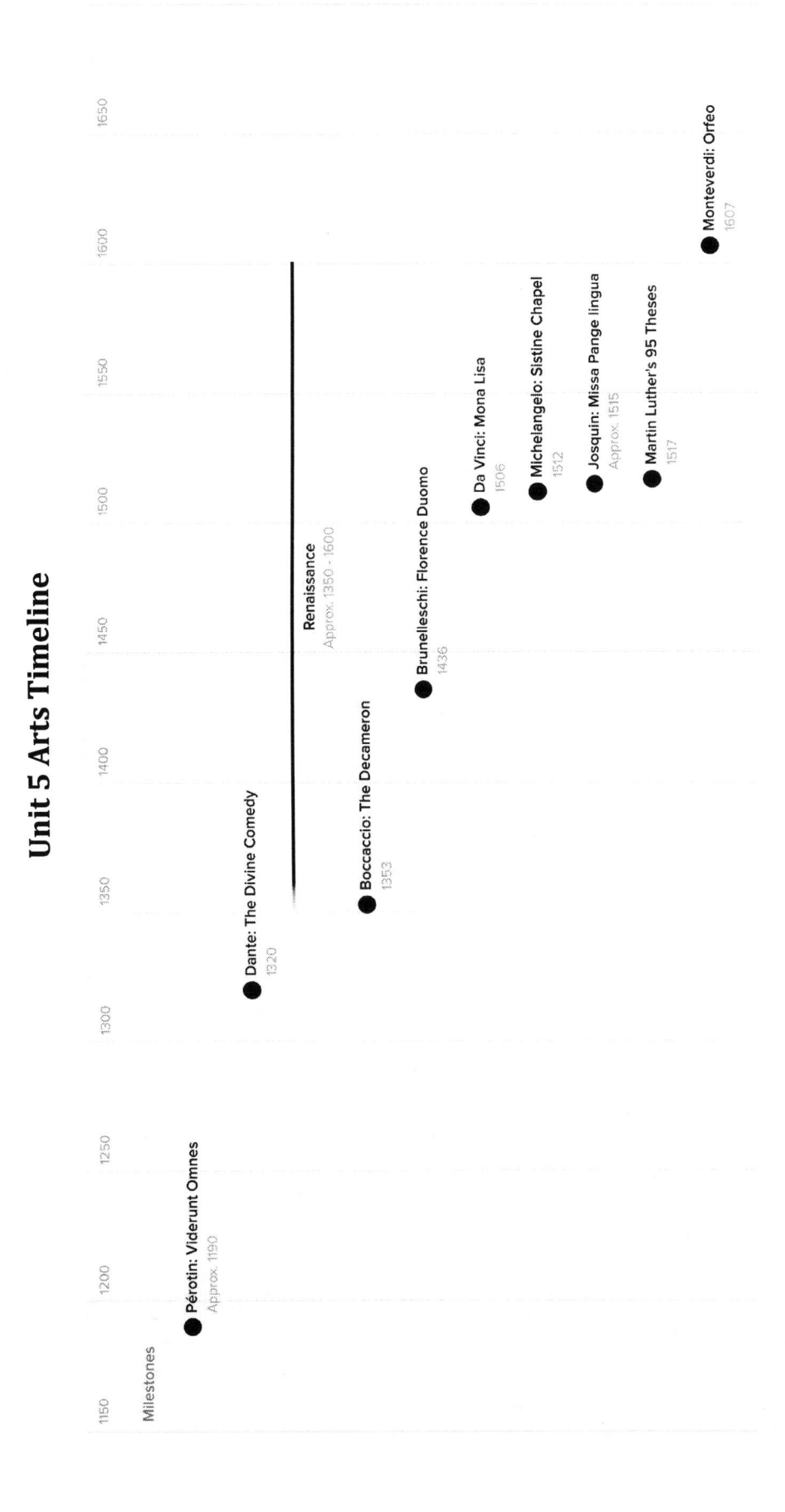

Unit 5: Sweeping Away the Renaissance into the Baroque

Unit 5 Arts Timeline

Milestones

- **Pérotin: Viderunt Omnes** — Approx. 1190
- **Dante: The Divine Comedy** — 1320
- **Boccaccio: The Decameron** — 1353
- **Brunelleschi: Florence Duomo** — 1436
- **Da Vinci: Mona Lisa** — 1506
- **Michelangelo: Sistine Chapel** — 1512
- **Josquin: Missa Pange lingua** — Approx. 1515
- **Martin Luther's 95 Theses** — 1517
- **Monteverdi: Orfeo** — 1607

Renaissance: Approx. 1350 – 1600

YOUR TIMELINE

Dates →

Unit 6

Liturgical Calendar, Street Parties, and the New Church Music

PEOPLE

Handel
Georg Friedrich
1685-1759
Baroque
Germany/Italy/England
Composer

Buxtehude
Dietrich
1637-1707
Baroque
Germany
Composer

Telemann
Georg Philipp
1681-1767
Baroque
Germany
Composer

Corelli
Arcangelo
1653-1713
Baroque
Italy
Composer

George I
George I of Hanover
1660-1727
Baroque
England
King

Carissimi
Giacomo
1605-1674
Baroque
Italy
Composer

Neri
Philip

1515-1595
Renaissance

Italian
Priest

PLACES

Bologna, Italy	44°29'41.59" N 11°20'33.42" E
London, England	51°30'26.46" N 0°07'39.93" W
Rio de Janeiro, Brazil	22°54'24.65" S 43°10'22.43" W
New Orleans, Louisiana	29°57'26.78" N 90°03'46.61" W

VOCABULARY

Liturgical (from the Greek λειτουργί leitourgia) (*leitos* = public) + (*ergos* = that works, performs, does)
The schedule of services—religious celebrations—that mark the progression of the church year. The "liturgical" calendar maintains a year-round schedule of the liturgies, or worship services, that should be observed.

Advent
The period of the liturgical calendar marked by the four Sundays leading up to Christmas Eve.

Lent
The forty days of fasting and preparation prior to Easter (excluding Sundays, which are always Feast Days).

Weiberfasnacht
A popular secular celebration, also known as *giovedí grasso* in Italian. Held the Thursday before Ash Wednesday, there are various traditions for celebrating. In some countries, for example, women enjoy cutting the necktie of any man found wearing one.

Rosenmontag
Also known as "Rose Monday" in English, this is the Monday before Ash Wednesday. Many cities stage lavish parades on this day, featuring floats bedecked with flowers.

Mardi gras (*mardi* = Tuesday) + (*gras* = fat)
Also known as *Fasnacht* in German, and "Shrove Tuesday" or "Fat Tuesday" in English. This is the Tuesday just before Ash Wednesday (the beginning of Lent) marking the last big celebration day of Carnival. Pancakes dripping in butter and syrup are traditionally associated with this day.

Carnival (*carne* = meat) + (*vale* = farewell). Also *Carnaval* and *Carnevale*.
Known as **Fasching** in German, Carnival is an unofficial period marking the celebrations that lead up to Ash Wednesday and the forty days of Lenten fasting before Easter. It is a fully secular tradition, not part of the Liturgical Calendar, and has ancient roots in pre-Christian Europe.

Oratorio
From the Italian verb to beseech, beg, or pray, *orare*. The oratorio is a musical setting of a text, primarily biblical or sacred. Developed at the end of the Renaissance, early sacred oratorios would be performed in a section of the church apart from the sanctuary known as the *Oratorium*—a hall for prayer and preaching, something like today's Sunday School Room. The oratorio during the Baroque period grew into a form of popular entertainment appropriate to the Lenten season. Like an opera, the oratorio begins with text, or a libretto, that is set to music for soloists, chorus, and instrumental ensemble. Unlike opera, however, oratorio is not "staged" (no costumes, acting, or sets).

Passion
Similar in many ways to the oratorio (not staged or acted), a "passion" is a dramatic choral work based specifically on the story of Christ's crucifixion and his suffering.

Cantata
From the Italian *cantare*, "to sing." This musical genre became very popular during the Baroque era as a principal form of sacred music. Setting texts in the vernacular, these were popular with Italian composers. The cantata was also integrated enthusiastically into the new Protestant (Lutheran) church services.

DATES

1710	Handel leaves Germany for England.
1714-1727	Reign of King George I, England
1715	Louis XIV dies.
1718	New Orleans founded.

1730	Benjamin Franklin begins to publish *Poor Richard's Almanack*.
1733	Georgia, the last of the thirteen American colonies, founded.
1739	Handel's oratorio *Saul* has its premiere.
1742	Handel's oratorio *Messiah* has its premiere in Dublin, Ireland.

LISTENING

See Listening Guide at http://www.professorcarol.com/dm-listening

Listening selections for this unit focus on vocal genres of the late Baroque (oratorio and cantata) and the works of Handel.

PUTTING IT ALL TOGETHER

1. Find descriptions of the characteristics and personalities of the following commedia dell'arte personalities:

   - Harlequin
   - Pantalone
   - Capitano
   - Brighella
   - Columbina
   - Pulcinella

   Also: What character was *El Medico dea Peaste [Peste]*? What kind of costume was worn? Why? What was the practical purpose for wearing masks during Carnival (why was it helpful to be disguised)?

2. Study the life of Handel. What kind of musical training did he receive? Did he come from a musical family? Look carefully at the genres of music that he composed: was he equally capable of composing both sacred and secular music? How many operas did he write? Why and when did he change his focus to oratorios?

3. Spend some time getting acquainted with the liturgical calendar. Depending upon your denomination and/or religion, you will probably see many feasts and celebrations that are familiar to you—maybe you know them all! Calculate which liturgical season is current while studying this unit. What do you know about it? What influence does the liturgical calendar have on the colors used inside the church (on the altar, or on the stole the pastor/priest will wear)?

4. Do people in your community celebrate Mardi Gras/Carnival? If so, how? What are the popular traditions? Who organizes the festivities? Is it a draw for tourism? If not, why not? If it is not celebrated where you live, try to determine the nearest place to your home where Carnival is celebrated.

VIEWING GUIDE

1. A text is considered _____ if the story deals with a religious theme, and _____ if it is concerned primarily with worldly (non-church) topics. Purely instrumental music (without text) can be considered "sacred" if _____
_____.

2. Martin Luther allegedly uttered, "Why should the Devil get all of the good tunes?" because _____
_____.

3. In a Christian context, a liturgy is a general term for _____
_____. In Eastern Christianity (Orthodoxy), a liturgy always means a service that celebrates _____.

4. A liturgical calendar lays out _____. Some celebrations have fixed dates, like _____, and others are linked to the lunar calendar, like _____
_____.

5. Theaters were traditionally closed in the summertime because _____
_____, but they were closed during Lent because _____
_____.

6. When faced with the prospect of a long period of fasting, people tended to _____. That made the pre-Lenten season an obvious season for performances of _____.
Why? _____
_____. In addition, people attended _____.

7. In the United States, Carnival, or *Mardi gras*, is celebrated with great gusto in _____ (city) because _____
_____

_____.

8. For each Carnival season, composers prepared _____. For the Lenten season, the same composers would write _____. Why? _____.

9. An oratorio was not performed inside of the _____. A cantata could be sacred or secular, and the sacred ones were indeed performed _____ (in what context?).

10. Oratorios were initially in _____ parts, and in the middle was a _____.

11. Stories from the (circle one) Old Testament / New Testament make the best oratorio topics because _____ _____.

12. Dramatic choral works that tell the story of Christ's crucifixion are called _____.

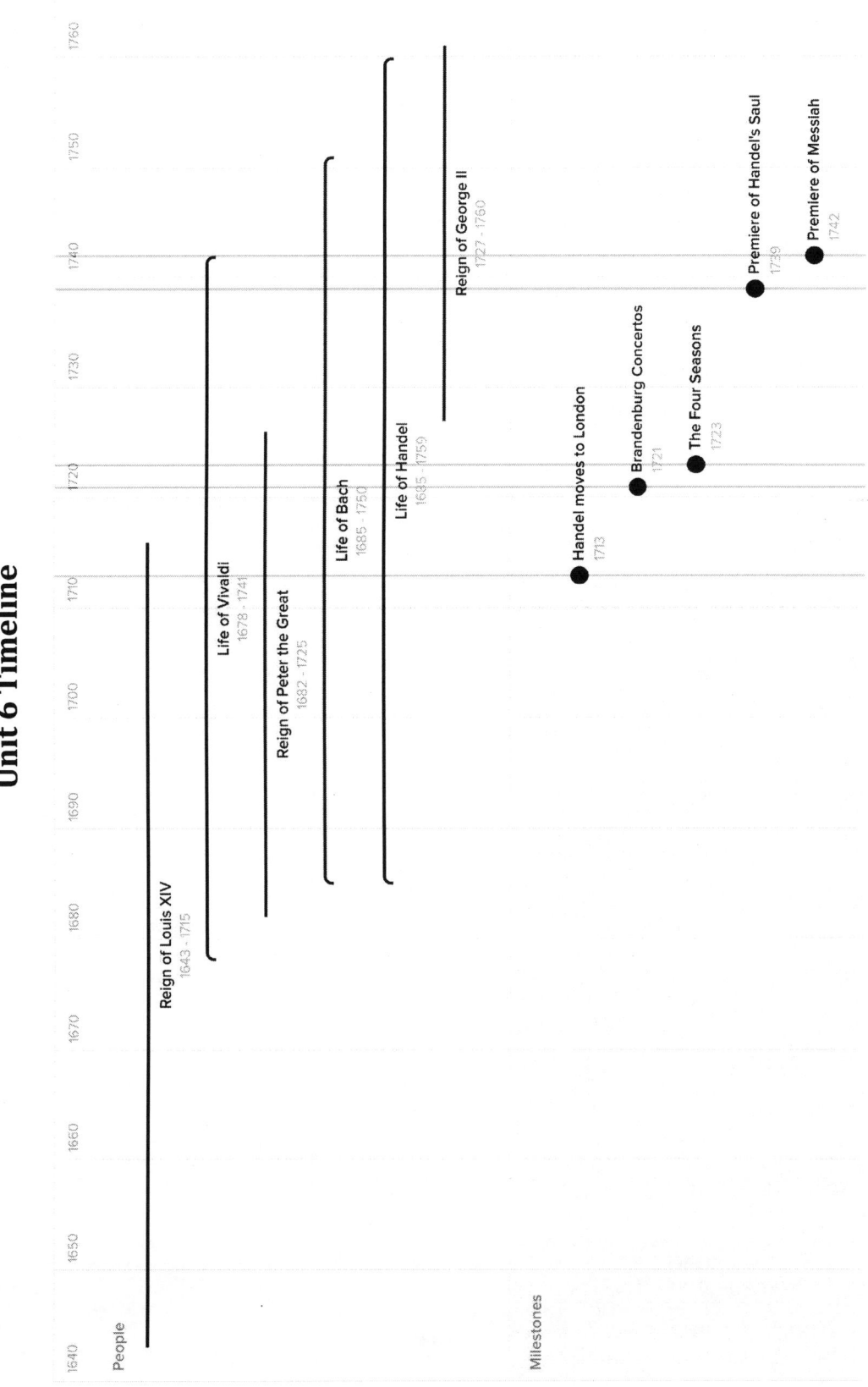

Unit 6: Liturgical Calendar, Street Parties, and the New Church Music 77

Unit 6 Timeline

People

- Reign of Louis XIV — 1643-1715
- Life of Vivaldi — 1678-1741
- Reign of Peter the Great — 1682-1725
- Life of Bach — 1685-1750
- Life of Handel — 1685-1759
- Reign of George II — 1727-1760

Milestones

- Handel moves to London — 1713
- Brandenburg Concertos — 1721
- The Four Seasons — 1723
- Premiere of Handel's Saul — 1739
- Premiere of Messiah — 1742

YOUR TIMELINE

Dates →

Unit 7

A Lively Journey Through the Life of Johann Sebastian Bach

PEOPLE

Bach
Johann Sebastian

1685-1750
Baroque

Germany
Composer

Handel
Georg Friedrich

1685-1759
Baroque

Germany/Italy/England
Composer

Telemann
Georg Philipp

1681-1767
Baroque

Germany
Composer

Vivaldi
Antonio

1678-1741
Baroque

Italy
Composer

Buxtehude
Dietrich

1637-1707
Baroque

Germany
Composer

Bach
Carl Philipp Emanuel

1714-1788
Baroque

Germany
Composer

Bach
Johann Christian

1735-1782
Baroque

Germany/England
Composer

PLACES

Eisenach	50°58'28.96" N 10°19'10.37" E
Ohrdruf	50°49'38.69" N 10°44'02.77" E
Lüneberg	53°14'47.12" N 10°24'41.46" E
Arnstadt	50°50'01.73" N 10°56'43.20" E
Lübeck	53°51'55.68" N 10°41'11.61" E
Mühlhausen	51°12'35.51" N 10°27'25.56" E
Weimar	50°58'46.18" N 11°19'24.76" E
Köthen	51°45'13.57" N 11°58'36.74" E
Leipzig (Thomaskirche)	51°20'20.72" N 12°22'21.96" E
Sanssouci Palace	52°24'15.13" N 13°02'18.60" E

VOCABULARY

Doctrine of Affections
Known in German as *Affektenlehre* (*Affekt* = affect or emotion) + (*Lehre* = teaching), the Doctrine of Affections was an important foundation of Baroque aesthetics, especially as applied to arts. According to the theory, an art like music was capable of "affecting" the hearer in powerful ways. Because of this power, music should express one consistent affect (or emotion) throughout each given section or movement rather than shifting from one affect to another.

Pastorale
From the Latin pastor, or shepherd. Music reflecting a "pastoral affect" had a calm and peaceful sound, reminding listeners of shepherds in green pastures, herding sheep (a favorite theme of painters and poets in the Renaissance and Baroque periods). Any movement entitled Pastorale was intended to evoke images of flocks grazing under the

protective eye of a shepherd in a beautiful natural setting.

Siciliano
Another common style or "affect" of Baroque music. Movements marked *Siciliano* were also "pastoral," with a lilting rhythm, and frequently in a minor key.

Collegia Musica
Informal groups of "musical colleagues" who would meet to discuss and play music together. These groups formed increasingly in the Baroque era and laid part of the groundwork for what ultimately would become public concerts.

Sanssouci
From the French *sans souci* (*sans* = without) + (*souci* = troubles), this was the name of Frederick the Great's palace in Potsdam, outside of Berlin, sometimes called his "Pleasure Palace." Sanssouci was designed as a royal get-away and a small version of Versailles, the famous French royal palace. Frederick himself designed many aspects of his palace and the surrounding park. In 1991, his remains were finally returned to Sanssouci to fulfill his wish to be buried next to his beloved greyhounds.

DATES

1640-1659	English Civil War
1660	English Monarchy restored
1678	Antonio Vivaldi is born.
1681	Pennsylvania founded by William Penn.
1682	Rene-Robert La Salle explores the lower Mississippi Valley region, claims it for France, and names it "Louisiana."
1685	J.S. Bach is born. Also born this year: Georg Friedrich Handel and Alessandro Scarlatti.
1750	Death of J.S. Bach
1754-1763	The French and Indian War (fought in America)
1756-1763	Seven Years' War (fought in Europe)

LISTENING

See Listening Guide at http://www.professorcarol.com/dm-listening

A brief survey of Bach's music hardly does it justice, but we offer here a sampling of different genres.

PUTTING IT ALL TOGETHER

■ ● ▲ ⬢ 1. Using the map of your choice and the list of "PLACES," trace the routes that Sebastian Bach would have traveled between his stations. Begin by marking each station and labeling the years that Bach spent there, then draw a line directly from the first station to the next. Try to imagine what these journeys would have been like. You may even want to discover the modern-day population of each of these cities. How do these cities associate themselves today with Bach's legacy? Below is the list of cities and years:

- Eisenach: 1685-1695
- Ohrdruf: 1695-1700
- Lüneberg: 1700-1702
- Arnstadt: 1703-1707
- Mühlhausen: 1707-1708
- Weimar: 1708-1717
- Köthen: 1717-1722
- Leipzig: 1723-1750

■ ● ▲ ⬢ 2. Antonio Vivaldi was a very popular Baroque composer with a high-profile career. Research Vivaldi and answer the following questions for both Vivaldi and J.S. Bach.

- What was each composer's chief instrument?

- In addition to composing, what musical job did each hold?

- Though both composers were teachers, did they teach boys or girls? (or) What was different about each teaching assignment/position?

- By which church (Protestant/Catholic) was each employed?

- What were the cities like where each man spent significant numbers of years? (You may need to do a little research on Venice in order to answer this question!)

- For what kinds of ensembles did each composer write?

- What kind of ensemble did each composer seem to prefer? Why do you think so?

- Did either composer compose operas? Are they well known?

- Finally, how prominent, or famous, was either composer during his lifetime?

Unit 7: A Lively Journey Through the Life of Johann Sebastian Bach

3. Although parts of Vivaldi's first concerto of *The Seasons* are heard on recordings in many places, such as in restaurants and television commercials, all four of these concerti are even more fabulous works to hear performed in an actual concert!

Take time to read each one of the sonnets that Vivaldi wrote to accompany his four concerti. Then listen to that concerto. Listen to a recorded performance. Think about how the titles of the movements, and the music itself, will depict the images in the sonnets.

4. By now you already know some things about Sebastian Bach's biography. Study the biographical information on Dieterich Buxtehude; you may even wish to investigate how to join the International Buxtehude Society and what activities it offers. What relationship did Buxtehude have to Bach, and why did Bach turn down Buxtehude's job? The answer may surprise you!

5. Research the lives of Bach's two most famous sons, C.P.E. and J.C. Bach:

- For what careers did each begin his advanced education and training?

- Which brother was older? How old was each when Sebastian Bach died?

- Which brother converted to Catholicism?

- In what genres of composition did each brother specialize? Remember: this is a direct reflection of the positions each held!

- Which brother wrote an important "treatise" on playing a particular instrument?

- Which brother had an influence on W.A. Mozart?

- Which was known as the "London" Bach and why?

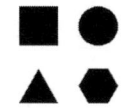

6. Learn more about each of the three stylistic designations below. How are they applied to art, design, literature, and music? How would you describe each of them to a friend who did not know anything about the topic? Place approximate dates for each on a blank "Timeline." Remember that any kind of style gains and falls in popularity gradually — there is not an "official" date at which something becomes "in" or "out" of style:

- Rococo

- Stil galant

- Empfindsamer stil (Empfindsamkeit)

84 DISCOVERING MUSIC STUDENT WORKBOOK

VIEWING GUIDE

1. It is useful to call Bach by his _____ name, _____, since so many males in his family had the same _____ name of _____.

2. The _____ of the _____ was a very broad idea used to organize Baroque expression and aesthetics. In short, something that started joyfully should _____ and not _____ _____.

3. We speak of Bach's various towns of residence/employment as his _____. He did move around a lot, but usually because he ____ _____.

4. In his job in the town where his cousin Johann Gottfried Walther worked, _____, Bach was primarily a _____ _____, but he got in trouble there because _____ _____.

5. In his next job at _____, he was writing music in the latest secular styles, which pleased him, but that job came to an end when _____ _____.

6. Bach's longest-lasting job was in _____ and his duties there included teaching and conducting the _____ at a church called _____. He also got very involved in music performed at the trendy _____. Those early groups of people who met to play music in public places were laying the foundation for what we will later call the _____.

7. The most technologically advanced instrument of the era (indeed one of the most technologically advanced objects of any kind) was the _____. It was powered by _____ who pumped the _____ to drive _____ through the _____ _____. Today that function is accomplished by _____.

8. The _____ was a small basic keyboard instrument that many people could afford. It (circle one) was / was not appropriate for public performance because _____. Its appeal lay in the fact that, at an individual key level, the player could _____ _____.

9. One of Bach's most successful sons, _____, worked for the German King _____ at the court in _____ (city). This king loved the new keyboard instrument ___ _____. He was also a marvelous flute player.

Unit 7 Timeline

Stations

- **Eisenach** — March 21, 1685 - March 2, 1695
- **Ohrdruf** — March 3, 1695 - 1699
- **Lüneburg** — 1700 - July 1702
- **Arnstadt** — August 1703 - June 1707
- **Mühlhausen** — July 1707 - June 1708
- **Weimar** — 1709 - 1717
- **Köthen** — December 6, 1717 - May 12, 1723
- **Leipzig** — May 13, 1723 - July 28, 1750

Personal Life

- **Marriage to Maria Barbara** — October 17, 1707 - July 7, 1720
- **Marriage to Anna Magdalena** — December 3, 1721 - July 28, 1750

Unit 7: A Lively Journey Through the Life of Johann Sebastian Bach 87

YOUR TIMELINE

Dates →

Unit 8

Enlightenment, Classicism, and the Astonishing Mozart

PEOPLE

Bach
Johann Christian
1735-1782
Baroque

Germany/England
Composer

Bach
Carl Philipp Emanuel
1714-1788
Baroque

Germany
Composer

Mozart
Leopold
1719-1787
Classical

Austria
Musician

Mozart
Wolfgang Amadeus
1756-1791
Classical

Austria
Composer

Haydn
Joseph
1732-1809
Classical

Austria
Composer

Rameau
Jean-Philippe
1683-1764
Baroque

France
Composer

Unit 8: Enlightenment, Classicism, and the Astonishing Mozart   89

Köchel
Ludwig
1800-1877
Classical

Austria
Musicologist

Cristofori
Bartolomeo
1655-1731
Renaissance

Italian
Instrument Maker

Quantz
Johann
1697-1773
Baroque

Germany
Composer

Frederick II
Frederick the Great
1712-1786
Baroque

Prussia
Emperor

Watteau
Antoine
1684-1721
Classical

France
Artist

Rousseau
Jean-Jacques
1712-1778
Classical

Switzerland, France
Philosopher

Voltaire
François-Marie Arouet
1694-1778
Classical

France
Writer

Diderot
Denis
1713-1784
Baroque

France
Enclycopedist

D'Alembert
Jean
1717-1783
Baroque

France
Enclycopedist

Jefferson
Thomas
1743-1826
Classical

United States
President

Da Ponte
Lorenzo
1749-1838
Classical

Italy, United States
Librettist

Beaumarchais
Pierre
1732-1799
Classical

France
Playwright

Louis XVI
1754-1793
Classical

France
King

Joseph II
1741-1790
Classical

Austria
Holy Roman Emperor

PLACES

Paris, France	48°51'23.81" N 2°21'08.00" E
Vienna, Austria	48°12'29.43" N 16°22'25.75" E
Prague, Czech Republic	50°04'31.94" N 14°26'16.08" E
Istanbul, Turkey	41°00'29.66" N 28°58'42.09" E

VOCABULARY

Classical
From the Latin noun *classicus*, meaning first or upper class. A term used to describe European art and architecture starting in the second half of the 18th century. Many of the artistic principles date back to Classical Antiquity.

Fortepiano
From the Italian words *forte* (strong, or loud) and *piano* (usually rendered "soft"—although another meaning is "smooth" or "graceful"). The instrument was also called a *pianoforte*. The word *"forte"* dropped away, leaving the name "piano." The *fortepiano* is the direct ancestor of the modern piano, and took its name from the fact that it was capable of playing both loudly and softly at the individual key level—something harpsichords and organs cannot do. The main feature of a *fortepiano* mechanism (action) is a hammer that strikes a string.

Rococo
From the French *rocaille*, meaning "debris" or "rubble." This style of fanciful early 18th-century art, architecture, and music reflected irregular but proportional natural shapes. Shells, pebbles, and vines are common decorative images in Rococo style.

Stil galant (*stil* = style)
From the French *galer*, meaning "to make merry" or "to make a show." This style of mid-18th-century art and architecture is reflected in paintings of what has been coined in this course as "clean sheep parties" or *fêtes galantes*, in which nobility would enjoy an idealized and cleaned-up version of "ordinary" natural life, accompanied by refreshments and dancing.

Empfindsamkeit (*Empfind* = sensitive) + (*sam* = ly) + (*keit* = ness)
This German word for "sensitivity" lends its name to *Empfindsamer Stil*, a style of music that was characteristic of the transition from Baroque to Romanticism. Music of this "style" featured sudden shifts from one "affect" (or emotion) to the next, evoking the sort of sudden changes one would find in the natural world (such as in weather, or in human nature!).

Sturm und Drang (*Sturm* = storm) + (*und* = and) + (*Drang* = stress: from *dringen*, to press, urge, come through)
Usually translated "storm and stress." The term comes from a literary movement that originated in Germany during the 1760s. Any art described as *Sturm und Drang* puts emphasis on psychological aspects, emotional affects, and the complexity of human nature.

Encyclopédists
This group of French scholars revived and further developed the ancient Greek fascination with collecting and organizing information. Its members included Diderot, Voltaire, and D'Alembert, as well as several others. They reflected a common Enlightenment ideal that education and knowledge would, in and of themselves, solve humanity's problems.

Divertimento
A composition for instrumental ensemble with several short movements, designed to be a light "diversion."

Köchel number
Mozart died before he could properly organize his compositions, plus many of his compositions had never been published. So any opus numbers attached to his pieces weren't sufficient. For that reason, a 19th-century German scholar named Ludwig Köchel undertook the huge task of putting Mozart's works into order and assigned them a "K." number. This kind of posthumous organization is necessary for many composers, and that's why, when you look at a concert program, or the contents of a recording, you find a variety of initials and complex letter/number designations after many composers' works.

Opera buffa
A type of opera that became very popular starting in the mid 18th century. *Opera buffa* had pleasant and funny plots, with lighter and more appealing styles of arias, in contrast to the serious plots and virtuosic arias of *opera seria*.

Drama giocoso
Mozart's own fusion of *opera seria* and *buffa*, this term was used for his opera *Don Giovanni*, which had several "layers" of story and meaning happening at one time. Although the layers all relate to one another and often feature the same characters, some layers are serious (deadly, even) while others are silly and romantic.

DATES

1754	The Oriental Academy opens in Vienna, Austria.
1761	Haydn begins his employment for Prince Paul Anton Esterhàzy.
1783	The American Revolutionary War ends.
1786	*Marriage of Figaro* has its premiere in Vienna.
1787	*Don Giovanni* has its premiere in Prague.
1789	The French Revolution begins.
1793	King Louis XVI and Queen Marie Antoinette executed.

Unit 8: Enlightenment, Classicism, and the Astonishing Mozart

1794	Eli Whitney receives a patent for the cotton gin.
1798	Premiere of Haydn's *The Creation*
1800	Seat of American government moves from Philadelphia to Washington, D.C. The Library of Congress founded.

LISTENING

See Listening Guide at http://www.professorcarol.com/dm-listening

Selections for this Unit will help to demonstrate the new simpler styles that replaced the complex Baroque textures, the transition from harpsichord to pianoforte, and the mature Classical style of Haydn and Mozart.

PUTTING IT ALL TOGETHER

1. Who were the Encyclopédists? Study the lives of Voltaire, Diderot, and Rousseau. What beliefs did they contribute to the "Enlightenment"? How did these beliefs contribute to the French and American Revolutions? In what different ways did Enlightenment thinkers define "nature," and where did human beings fit into nature?

2. Study the life of Thomas Jefferson. What were some of his greatest achievements? For which achievements did he, personally, wish to be remembered? To what important American documents did he contribute? Which parts of Europe did Jefferson visit? What instrument did he play? Was he well-versed in literature and the arts? What can you see if you visit Monticello today?

3. Although best known in history as "Wolfgang's father," Leopold Mozart was a successful and well-respected musician during his lifetime (perhaps even more "respected" than his son!). What instrument was at the center of Leopold's life, and how did this influence the types of works he composed? What important book on playing an instrument did he write? What important contributions did he make to the lives of his children?

4. Read about the life of Mozart's favorite (eclectic!) librettist Lorenzo Da Ponte. Where did he get his name (he was not born "Lorenzo Da Ponte"), and which countries did he call home? How did he come to be associated with Mozart? Where did he go when he left Vienna? When did he move to the United States? What important work did he do in the United States? How many years did he outlive Mozart?

5. Choose an opera of Mozart, if possible one that is "famous" and also new to you. Become familiar with it and watch a complete performance. Find out what are its best-known arias. Look for performances of these arias by several different artists. Look for and try to describe the changes in performance style you are likely to hear in these various performances.

6. Compare and contrast the lives of Mozart and Haydn. For each composer, answer the following questions:

- What kind of early education did he receive?
- What kind of early musical training did he receive?
- Did he come from a musical family?
- Each had an "early" musical career, at a young age. How were those careers different?
- Which composer did the most traveling?
- Which composer had the steadiest employment?
- Which composer wrote the most operas? The most symphonies?
- Which composer wrote the most string quartets?
- How many children did each composer have?

VIEWING GUIDE

1. The unit begins with a comparison of the end of the Baroque era to the end of the Big Band Era after World War II. Points of similarity include _____ _____ _____.

2. The term _____ is problematic, because it has meanings far beyond a specific period of music during Mozart's lifetime.

3. A technique where the notes of a simple harmony are "activated" and played over and over, quickly, to energize the harmony is called _____ _____.

4. The eighteenth century is an era of Absolute _____, including Frederick the Great of _____, Catherine the Great of _____, and Joseph II of _____.

5. There was a royal passion for collecting _____

Unit 8: Enlightenment, Classicism, and the Astonishing Mozart

_____.

6. The term _____ came from a word meaning "rock debris" and featured natural designs like shells, leaves, and vines.

7. Art or music described as *Stil* _____ is characterized by _____. The painter _____ was so popular that even a new style of "natural" or informally draped clothing was named for him.

8. _____ is primarily a German 18th-century literary movement that stressed dark and emotional ideas, but the term was applied also to some music.

9. Another German term, *Empfindsamkeit*, means _____ style. It stood in direct contrast to the old aesthetic—the Doctrine of the _____—where all emotions were constant in an individual movement or section of music.

10. Bach's _____ were far more modern than he, and they embraced new ideas. One worked in Berlin for the _____ King named _____.

11. The _____ is an instrument with a very soft sound, and sensitive to the touch, but too soft to be suitable for public performance.

12. Three interesting features of a piano action, as demonstrated by Michael Inman at Steinway Hall: _____.

13. The _____ was associated with aristocracy in Europe, but the new keyboard instrument, the _____, was not. An ____ _____ has the same mechanism, but it's turned at a 90-degree angle to fit in a smaller space.

14. The most famous Enlightenment figure in America was _____ _____.

15. An Eastern-European city that embraced Mozart's music strongly: _____.

16. Mozart was Austrian-born, but his music was so often written in _____ style. This style dominated European music in the 18th

century. Only the country of _____ consistently resisted this style in favor of its own.

17. Mozart was fond of a newly invented (18th-century) wind instrument called the _____ and he wrote music for a well-known virtuoso who made his career on this instrument.

18. Europeans in the 18th century found anything _____ to be fashionable and exotic.

19. *Opera* _____ became more popular than *opera* _____ in Mozart's day. Spoken-dialogue operas called _____ were also popular. Mozart's _____ (German term) is a famous example.

20. Both Mozart and his librettist, _____, chose to set to music a French play that had been banned. The resulting opera was called _____.

21. Haydn had a different mentality than Mozart. For example, _____
_____
_____.

22. Haydn was a genius at writing _____ and wrote more than one hundred. He also wrote a great deal of music for the _____, a strange stringed instrument favored by his patron, the Count.

23. Haydn was very clever in how he set the words in his oratorio *The Creation*, especially the section _____.

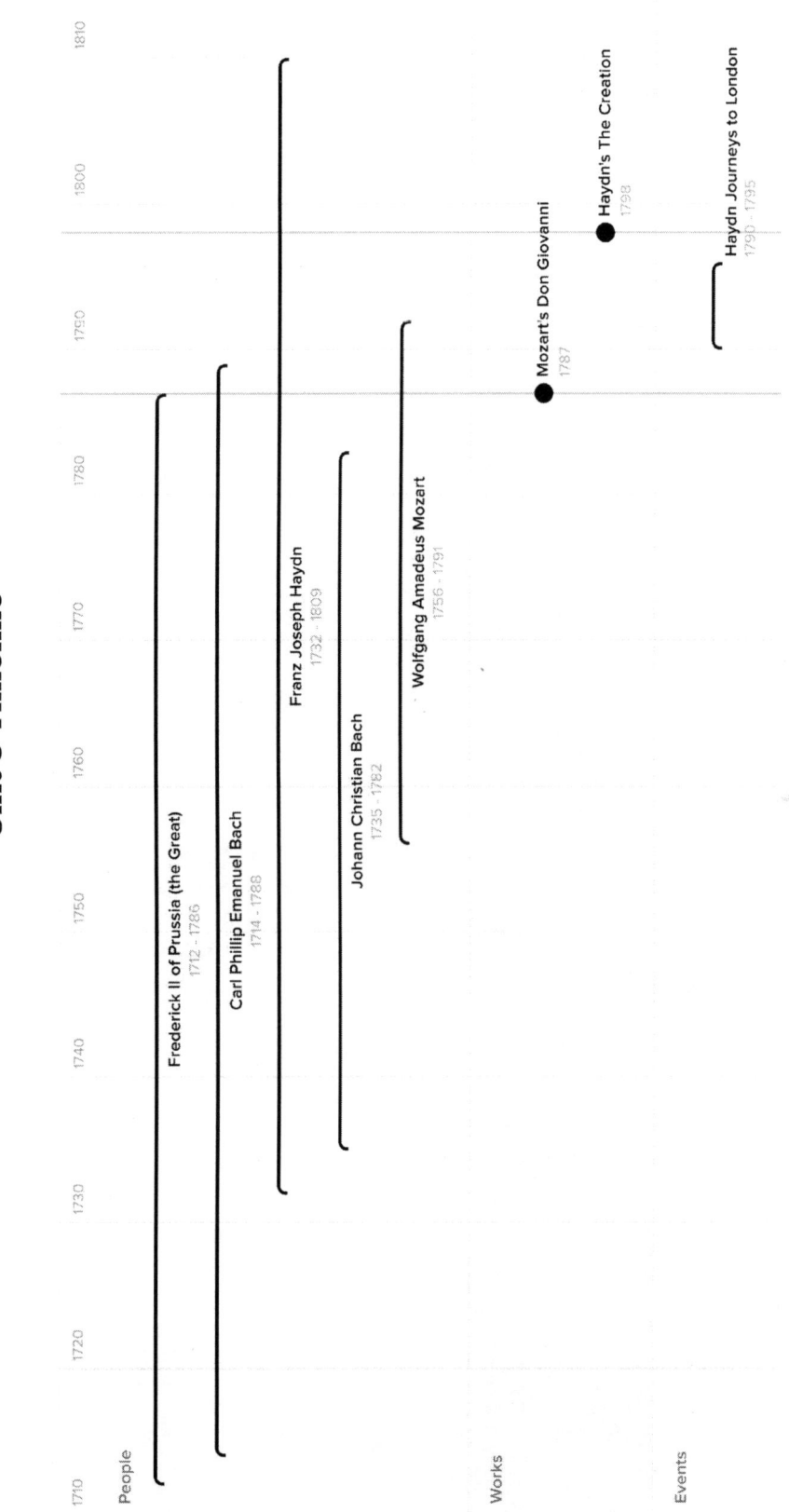

Unit 8: Enlightenment, Classicism, and the Astonishing Mozart

Unit 8 Timeline

People
- Frederick II of Prussia (the Great): 1712 - 1786
- Carl Phillip Emanuel Bach: 1714 - 1788
- Franz Joseph Haydn: 1732 - 1809
- Johann Christian Bach: 1735 - 1782
- Wolfgang Amadeus Mozart: 1756 - 1791

Works
- Mozart's Don Giovanni: 1787
- Haydn's The Creation: 1798

Events
- Haydn Journeys to London: 1790 - 1795

98 DISCOVERING MUSIC STUDENT WORKBOOK

YOUR TIMELINE

Dates ⟶

Unit 9

Into the Abyss: The Century Struggles with Unfettered Imagination

PEOPLE

Napoleon
Napoleon Bonaparte

1769-1821
Classical

France
Emperor

Goethe
Johann

1749-1832
Romantic

Germany
Writer

Schiller
Friedrich

1759-1805
Romantic

Germany
Writer

Beethoven
Ludwig

1770-1827
Classical/Romantic

Germany, Austria
Composer

Grimm
Jakob (1785-1863)
Wilhelm (1786-1859)

Romantic

England
Writers

Perrault
Charles

1623-1708
Baroque

French
Author

Joséphine
Joséphine Beauharnais Bonaparte

1763-1814
Classical

France
Empress

Shelley
Mary

1797-1851
Romantic

England
Writer

Friedrich
Caspar David

1759-1805
Romantic

Germany
Artist

Pushkin
Alexander

1799-1837
Romantic

Russia
Writer

Goya
Francisco

1746-1828
Romantic

Spain
Artist

Delacroix
Eugène

1798-1863
Romantic

France
Artist

Hoffmann
E.T.A.

1776-1822
Romantic

Germany
Writer

Poe
Edgar Allan

1809-1849
Romantic

United States
Writer

Unit 9: Into the Abyss: The Century Struggles with Unfettered Imagination

David
Jacques-Louis
1748-1825
Classical

France
Artist

Boethius
c. 480-c. 525
Medieval

Rome
Philosopher, Music Theorist

Scott
Walter
1771-1832
Romantic

Scotland
Writer

Coleridge
Samuel
1772-1834
Romantic

England
Writer

Byron
George Gordon
1788-1824
Romantic

England
Writer

Wackenroder
Wilhelm
1773-1798
Romantic

Germany
Writer

Tieck
Ludwig
1773-1853
Romantic

Germany
Writer

Menzel
Adolph
1815-1905
Romantic

German
Painter

Berlioz
Hector

1803-1869
Romantic

France
Composer

Herder
Johann Gottfried

1744-1803
Baroque

Germany
Theologian

PLACES

Weimar, Germany	50°58'46.18" N 11°19'24.76" E
Moscow, Russia	55°45'20.97" N 37°37'02.28" E
Elba, Italy	42°46'41.47" N 10°11'33.86" E
Paris, France	48°51'23.81" N 2°21'08.00" E
Corsica, France	42°02'22.58" N 9°00'46.41" E

VOCABULARY

Romanticism
A literary movement that focuses on imagination and human emotion. This movement spilled over into all of the arts. Consequently, the term refers both to an era in European cultural history (the 19th century) and to an aesthetic approach that leaves behind the logic and rationalism found in the Enlightenment.

Gemütlichkeit
Defined as "good nature, friendliness, coziness," this unique German term comes from the noun *Gemüt*, or "heart, mind, feeling." It refers to the general atmosphere in German culture as people recovered from the trauma of the Napoleonic Wars. The values projected were introspective, homey, and amiable.

Biedermeier
Originally a term used to describe a particular style of furniture popular in 19th-century Vienna, Biedermeier describes the clean lines and classical elements popular in all kinds of art and architecture between the end of the Napoleonic Wars (1815) and the beginning of the pan-European revolutionary period (1848). These elements complemented a wider social phenomenon that focused upon home and family—the rising middle class—rather than nobility and privilege.

Novel
A literary genre that began in the late 17th century, blossomed in the 18th century, and flourished during the Romantic era. Novels are fictional works that tell a story. They can be written in narrative form with dramatic (interactive) characters. Many early novels were written as an exchange of letters, called an epistolary novel. A short novel is called a novella.

Musica instrumentalis, musica humana, and musica mundana
Boethius' three divisions of music, from the physical to the divine: *Musica instrumentalis* is music of physical objects (instruments), *musica humana* is the music made by humans, such as by air (singing), and *musica mundana* is the music of the spheres.

DATES

1774	*The Sorrows of Young Werther* by Johann von Goethe
1788	U.S. Constitution ratified
1789	French Revolution
1789-1793	Reign of Terror
1797	John Adams innaugurated second U.S. President
1804	Coronation of Napoleon
1804-1806	Lewis and Clark Expedition
1805	Battle of Austerlitz
1808	*Faust* Part I by Johann von Goethe
1812	Battle of Borodino
1814	Napoleon exiled to Elba
1814-1815	Congress of Vienna
1815	Napoleon defeated in Battle of Waterloo
1818	*Frankenstein: A Modern Prometheus* by Mary Shelley
1819	*Ivanhoe* by Sir Walter Scott
1834	Slavery abolished in British Empire
1840-1860	Oregon Trail established as main highway to the Northwestern U.S.
1859	*A Tale of Two Cities* by Charles Dickens

104 DISCOVERING MUSIC STUDENT WORKBOOK

LISTENING

See Listening Guide at http://www.professorcarol.com/dm-listening

These listening selections offer an overview of some of the many styles and genres of the Romantic era.

VIEWING GUIDE

1. The first thing to realize about the Romantic era is how important _____ (art form) is, and always has been, to Europeans.

2. Romanticism developed in stages. First, in the early part of the 19th century, artists became fascinated by _____ _____. They also looked into their national _____ and collected their national _____. Using all this material, in a kind of Stage Three, they set about creating _____ _____.

3. The term Romantic or Romanticism means many things, including ___ _____ _____.

4. The English writer _____, in his novel _____ _____, gave one of the best literary portraits of the French Revolutionary period and the many difficult situations that followed. That novel opens with a famous line: _____ _____.

5. Napoleon may have come out of the new intellectual era focused on rationalism, known as _____, but it was the timeless urge to conquer and to grab power that led him to be _____ _____ at _____ Cathedral in 1804.

6. The painter _____ showed Napoleon in all his glory. But Napoleon's glory turned to ashes when he tried, ill-advisedly, to conquer Russia in _____ (year). The Russians survived, and then triumphed, by _____. The parallels in this campaign with a campaign waged by _____ in the 20th century are chilling.

Unit 9: Into the Abyss: The Century Struggles with Unfettered Imagination   105

7. After the Napoleonic Wars, people drew inward, seeking stability and comfort. A style of furnishing and art called _____ was launched. A fine German painter named _____ captured the mood well. There is even a German term for "cozy" that is used to describe this era: _____. Meanwhile, a long series of peace conferences called the _____ tried to put the Old Europe back together.

8. We can use the words from an 18th-century German novel called *Joseph Berlinger* to see how the new Romantic authors _____ _____ _____. Artists were definitely departing from a Classical view of music. In fact, suddenly the arts became _____ _____.

9. It's revealing to see the old three-part Greek view of music, starting at the top with _____ (music of the _____), followed by _____ (music made by human beings), and finally _____ (music made by physical objects like instruments).

10. The German writer _____ idolized the composer _____. In his writings, he describes music in very emotional language with words like _____. His stories are often about musicians, but his most famous story is known to us as _____.

11. Another writer who packed a power-punch was the English novelist _____. His novels were huge hits. Then there was the Romantic English poet _____. He died quite young. He, like the composer _____, was fascinated by the story of *Don Juan*, or, in Italian, *Don Giovanni*.

12. The German writers known as _____ collected and published volumes of important fairy tales. Fairy tales really aren't designed just for children, because _____ _____.

13. Maybe the most famous novel about the "supernatural" in the 19th century was Mary Shelley's _____ in 1818. And the most famous American poem about a spooky threatening bird, _____ _____, was written by the great American Romantic writer _____.

14. The Romantic era was also a time when people began to research and understand the problem of _____ (medical condition) better. Sir Walter Scott incorporated this theme in his novels, including one that became the plot for a famous opera _____.

15. But the most significant of all the Romantic writers was arguably a German author named _____. He became famous in his twenties when he wrote a short novel called _____. It was essentially the story of a love triangle, carried forth as a novel in "letter" form, which we call an _____. But this one was strange because the letters went only _____. The story ends with the _____ of the main character _____.

16. Goethe got invited to live in _____ (city), and he went, living quite (circle one) poorly / well for the rest of his life. There he wrote over many years the most significant work of his career, the play _____. The entire Part I of this work turns on a _____ that the Professor makes with the _____. At issue is whether or not the _____ can grant the Professor one moment of _____. If so, the _____ wins his _____.

17. Another great German poet and playwright living in the same city towards the end of the above-mentioned writer's life was _____.

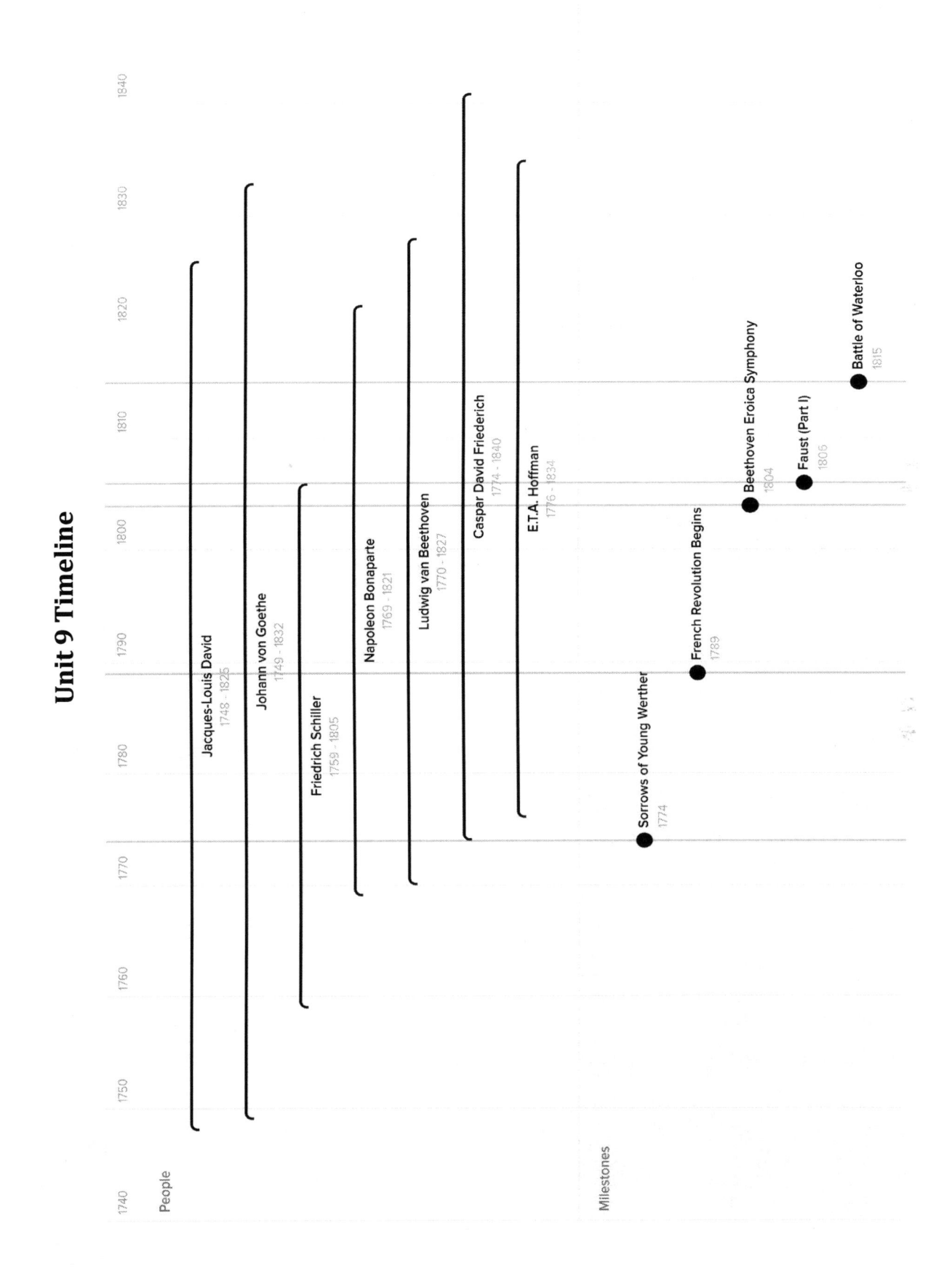

Unit 9: Into the Abyss: The Century Struggles with Unfettered Imagination

Unit 9 Timeline

People

- Jacques-Louis David (1748 - 1825)
- Johann von Goethe (1749 - 1832)
- Friedrich Schiller (1759 - 1805)
- Napoleon Bonaparte (1769 - 1821)
- Ludwig van Beethoven (1770 - 1827)
- Caspar David Friederich (1774 - 1840)
- E.T.A. Hoffman (1776 - 1834)

Milestones

- Sorrows of Young Werther — 1774
- French Revolution Begins — 1789
- Beethoven Eroica Symphony — 1804
- Faust (Part I) — 1805
- Battle of Waterloo — 1815

108 DISCOVERING MUSIC STUDENT WORKBOOK

YOUR TIMELINE

Dates →

Unit 10

Beethoven as Hero and Revolutionary

PEOPLE

Beethoven
Ludwig
1770-1827
Classical/Romantic

Germany, Austria
Composer

Napoleon
Napoleon Bonaparte
1769-1821
Classical

France
Emperor

Friedrich
Caspar David
1759-1805
Romantic

Germany
Artist

Herschel
William
1738-1822
Romantic

Germany
Astronomer

Zelter
Carl
1758-1832
Romantic

Germany
Composer

PLACES

Weimar, Germany	50°58'46.18" N 11°19'24.76" E
Bonn, Germany	50°44'12.90" N 7°06'04.32" E
Vienna, Austria	48°12'29.43" N 16°22'25.75" E
Heiligenstadt, Austria	48°15'17.33" N 16°21'21.98" E

VOCABULARY

Revolutionary
This adjective can be applied to anything that is related to, inspired by, or that brings about, revolution. Usually, revolution indicates the overthrowing of something, whether it is a government, or a long-held theory. For example, many nations have fought a "Revolutionary War," and many important scientific discoveries are the result of a "revolutionary" new idea.

Sturm und Drang (*Sturm* = storm) + (*und* = and) + (*Drang* = stress: from *dringen*, to press, urge, come through)
The *Sturm und Drang* aesthetic movement drew its name from the title of a novel, written in 1776 by German novelist Friedrich von Klinger. Works from this period reflect *Sturm und Drang* by portraying tremendous emotional upheaval, extremes of all kinds, and the struggle of the individual against social norms.

Monumentalism
This term applies to the late 19th-century tendency to create "monuments" of art that were epic in every sense of the word. In an effort to overwhelm the senses, large, long, oversized, powerful creative works appeared in every discipline.

Motive
An easily recognizable, repeating pattern in a work of art. In music, a motive consists of a short thematic statement that recurs as a unifying element of the music.

Beethovenian/Beethoveniana
A term applied to all things concerning Beethoven.

DATES

1768	Friedrich von Schiller writes a poem, part of which will become the text to the final movement of Beethoven's Symphony No. 9, Opus 125 (*Ode to Joy*).
1770	Beethoven's birth
1776	Friedrich von Klinger writes the novel *Sturm und Drang*.
	The American colonies declare independence from England.
	Thomas Paine publishes *Common Sense*.
1781	William Herschel discovers Uranus.
1787	Beethoven travels to Vienna to meet Mozart.
1789	French Revolution begins.
1792	Beethoven arrives in Vienna.
1802	Beethoven writes his *Heiligenstadt Testament*.
1803	Beethoven's Symphony No. 3 ("Eroica")
	Thomas Jefferson makes the "Louisiana Purchase" from France.
1804	Napoleon crowns himself Emperor of France.
1808	Beethoven's Symphony No. 6 ("Pastoral")
1812	America enters the War of 1812.
1824	Beethoven's Symphony No. 9, Op. 125
1827	Beethoven's death
1828	Andrew Jackson elected President of the United States.

LISTENING

See Listening Guide at http://www.professorcarol.com/dm-listening

Beethoven's monumentalism included expanding musical works to greater lengths. Recognizing that you may have time limitations, we suggest focusing on the first movement of the concerto, symphony, and string quartet, and listen to the remaining movements as time allows.

PUTTING IT ALL TOGETHER

1. Compare and contrast the French and American Revolutions. Consider the following points, including the French and American characteristics of each, and how/why those characteristics differ:

- Religious heritage

- Political traditions

- Day-to-day life for "ordinary" individuals

- Rural versus urban setting

- Foreign allegiances/relationships

2. Compare two performances of Beethoven's Violin Concerto. What differences can you describe between the two performances?

3. Spend some time researching the life and works of Goethe. Although he is best known today for his significant contributions to German literature, he was very knowledgeable about and interested in other areas. What was his most important scientific theory? What kind of education did he receive and for what profession? What kind of duties did he have in Weimar (remember, writing did not always pay his bills!)? Were all of Goethe's works based on plots developed by Goethe himself, or were they derived from other sources? You may even want to research some of the poets or other figures with whom he had close relationships. Create a smaller timeline that specifically draws parallels between Goethe's life and the major events of the American Revolution, as well as Beethoven's life.

4. A number of important American figures, including Thomas Jefferson, John Adams, and Benjamin Franklin, spent significant time in Europe during Beethoven's lifetime. Do you think Beethoven would have been sympathetic to the American cause? Why or why not? Which men served as U.S. President during Beethoven's life?

5. Explore the city of Bonn, Beethoven's birthplace. What is the city like today? What can you learn about the university? Bonn's cultural life? What role did Bonn play during the period that Germany was divided by the Wall (East and West Germany)? To what degree does Bonn seem to identify itself as Beethoven's Birthplace?

6. Learn what you can about Beethoven's Birth House in Bonn. Find out what it costs to visit, and what a visitor can see. See if you can locate information about a Beethoven Society (Gesellschaft). Would these be only in Germany? Austria? Worldwide? Also, explore the Ira F. Brilliant Center for Beethoven Studies in San Jose. What can you find there? Why did the collection and center cone into being?

Unit 10: Beethoven as Hero and Revolutionary

VIEWING GUIDE

1. Beethoven is famous not only for his music, but because _____.

2. When the French Revolution broke out, Beethoven was ____ years old.

3. Beethoven was the first significant composer to break away from _____.

4. Did Beethoven come from a musical family? _____.

5. What kind of challenges did Beethoven face when he moved to Vienna at age 22? _____.

6. Which highly celebrated, older author and thinker suggested some "polish" to Beethoven's manners and professional demeanor? _____. Did Beethoven take his suggestions? _____

7. How did Beethoven respond to Napoleon? _____.

8. What *kind* of opera was Beethoven's *Fidelio*? _____. How many overtures did he write for the opera? _____

9. *Fidelio*, which was supposedly based on a true story, presented realistic human problems, including _____.

10. As his deafness worsened, Beethoven's music became _____.

11. In Max Klinger's 1902 statue of Beethoven, the composer is depicted _____.

12. How is Klinger's statue of Beethoven a symbol of Beethoven's legacy? _____.

13. The city of Heiligenstadt literally means _____. Beethoven went there (why?) _____ _____. The strange letter he wrote there in 1802 is called the Heiligenstadt _____ and it's important in the study of Romanticism because _____ _____ _____.

14. Parks in the 19th century changed from _____ to ___ _____.

15. Particular features of Beethoven's music (especially when contrasted with Mozart's!) include _____ _____ _____.

16. How did Beethoven change traditional tempo (and expression) markings? _____ _____.

17. We can see Beethoven's creative process in his many pages of musical _____, which have helped to preserve his _____ _____.

18. List some of the reasons why Caspar David Friedrich used the moon so much in his paintings. _____ _____.

19. William Herschel was known as the _____, in part because he discovered _____.

Unit 10 Timeline

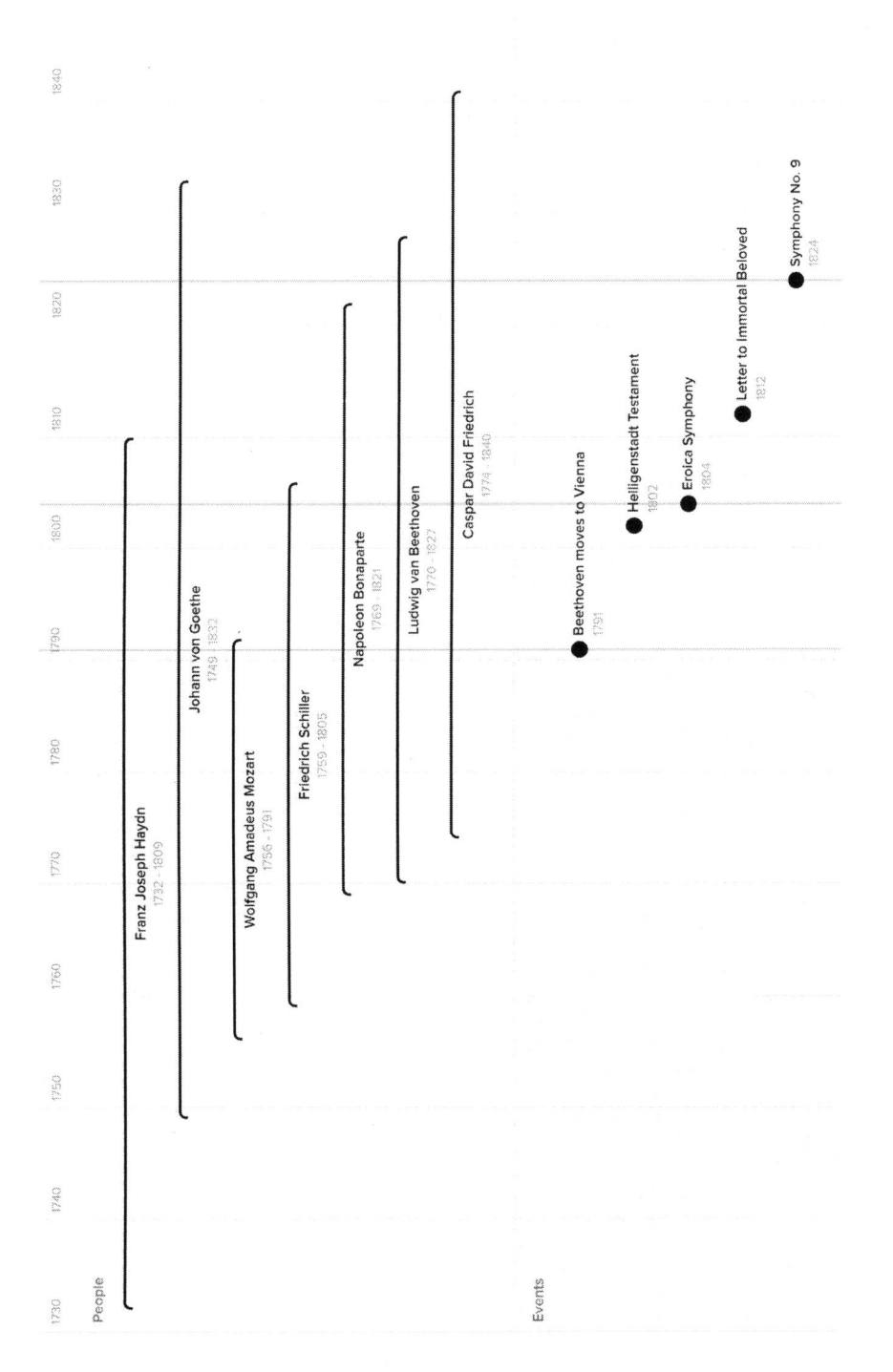

People

- Franz Joseph Haydn (1732 – 1809)
- Johann von Goethe (1749 – 1832)
- Wolfgang Amadeus Mozart (1756 – 1791)
- Friedrich Schiller (1759 – 1805)
- Napoleon Bonaparte (1769 – 1821)
- Ludwig van Beethoven (1770 – 1827)
- Caspar David Friedrich (1774 – 1840)

Events

- Beethoven moves to Vienna — 1791
- Heiligenstadt Testament — 1802
- Eroica Symphony — 1804
- Letter to Immortal Beloved — 1812
- Symphony No. 9 — 1824

116 DISCOVERING MUSIC STUDENT WORKBOOK

Dates ⟶ **YOUR TIMELINE** ⟶

Unit 11

Salons, Poetry, and the Power of Song

PEOPLE

Schubert
Franz
1797-1828
Romantic

Austria
Composer

Schumann
Robert
1810-1856
Romantic

Germany
Composer

Schumann
Clara Wieck
1819-1896
Romantic

Germany
Pianist, Composer

Loewe
Carl
1796-1869
Romantic

Germany
Composer

Heine
Heinrich
1797-1856
Romantic

Germany
Writer

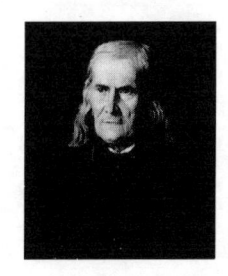

Rückert
Friedrich
1788-1866
Romantic

German
Poet

Müller
Wilhelm
1794-1827
Romantic

German
Poet

Goethe
Johann
1749-1832
Romantic

Germany
Writer

PLACES

Leipzig, Germany	51°20'10.53" N 12°22'59.80" E
Vienna, Austria	48°12'11.50" N 16°22'10.95" E
Loreley	50°08'21.00" N 7°43'41.00" E
Cologne, Germany	50°56'15.11" N 6°57'37.00" E

VOCABULARY

Lied
Plural *Lieder*. German for "song." This term is also specifically used for art songs based on German poetry composed from the late 18th century through the 19th century.

Liederkreis (*Lieder* = songs) + (*Kreis* = circle, or cycle)
A group of related poems turned into songs, set in a specific order, and intended to be performed together.

Bourgeoisie
The social class between the aristocracy and the working class. We are likely to call it the "middle" class. Growth of the middle class, or *bourgeoisie*, was a phenomenon of great importance in Europe during the late 18th century and the 19th century. These people will become the newest patrons of music in the 19th century, purchasing tickets to concerts and operas, and buying instruments and sheet music to play at home.

Gewandhaus (*Gewand* = garment/cloth) + (*Haus* = house)
This world-famous concert hall in Leipzig has been home to the celebrated Gewandhaus Orchestra for more than two centuries. The original building was home to Leipzig's fabric guild, until a group of Leipzig merchants founded a concert society and appropriated the hall for its use. The orchestra grew, and enjoyed many celebrated artistic directors, including Felix Mendelssohn. Today, housed in the third building to bear the name, the

Gewandhaus Orchestra is one of Europe's best.

Biedermeier
Originally a term used to describe a particular style of furniture popular in 19th-century Vienna, *Biedermeier* describes the clean lines and classical elements popular in all kinds of art and architecture between the end of the Napoleonic Wars (1815) and the beginning of the pan-European revolutionary period (1848). These elements complemented a wider social phenomenon that focused upon home and family—the rising middle class—rather than nobility and privilege.

Ballad
This type of poem, a dramatic narrative featuring different characters and much action, was a frequent source of texts for *Lieder*.

Erlkönig (*Erl* = Elf) + (*König* = king)
This ballad, based on a Danish legend, was written in 1782 by Goethe as part of a larger work, and subsequently set to music by a number of Romantic composers.

Dichterliebe (*Dichter* = poet) + (*Liebe* = love)
From a large collection of poems by Heinrich Heine, sixteen poems were chosen by Robert Schumann and turned into a cycle of songs about disappointed love.

Salon
While a salon could be just a particular room in one's home, salon was also the term applied to a gathering of people or the artistic events that took place during the gathering. Guests would be invited on a regular basis, and the newest poetry and music would be the focus of the social event. Salons had varying social status, depending on whose home it was, which guests came, and who the featured artists were.

Prima le parole, e dopo la musica
This Italian phrase translates, "First the words, and then the music," and it reminds us that both songs and dramatic vocal music (operas, oratorios, cantatas) begin with a text that forms the basis for the music.

DATES

1760-1820	Reign of England's King George III
1829	Louis Braille invents and alphabet and printing of it for the blind.
1834	Indian Territory organized in the U.S.
1838	Samuel Morse invents Morse Code.
1840	Robert and Clara Schumann are married.

1845	Elias Howe invents the sewing machine.
1854	Henry David Thoreau's *Walden*
1855	Walt Whitman's *Leaves of Grass*

LISTENING

See Listening Guide at http://www.professorcarol.com/dm-listening

Schubert and Schumann set the standard for German song for the generations to come: Johannes Brahms, Hugo Wolf, Gustav Mahler, etc. We also take a peek ahead at some of the late Romantic French *mélodie*.

PUTTING IT ALL TOGETHER

■ ● ▲ ⬢ 1. Now that you've taken a tour of Mendelssohn's salon in the Video Lecture for this unit, consider some of the design elements that made it especially comfortable for musical performances. Compare its current organization as an "official concert space" in the Mendelssohnhaus Museum (chairs lined up in stiff rows, piano at the front) with the salon in Kupelweiser's painting of Schubert. Consider the differences—which salon would be more suitable for a friendly gathering? Which seems more respectful to the performers? Which seems more appropriate for the early 19th century and why?

■ ● ▲ ⬢ 2. Make a list of five of your favorite songs (remember: unlike a "piece" of music, songs require words). Try to vary the time period from which they come. Consider the following:

• What is the topic of the song? (What is it about?) What is an appropriate setting for this song? To say it another way, in what kind of place might it first have been performed? (This may be difficult, since you most likely listened to this song on recorded media.)

• If you've heard a live performance, where or how did the song differ from the recorded version?

• If the song is accompanied, what kinds of instruments are used and how do they contribute to the effect of the song?

• Will these songs (in your opinion) still be well known and performed in 50 or 100 years? Of course, this will be speculation, but give an answer and support it with your reasoning.

Unit 11: Salons, Poetry, and the Power of Song **121**

3. Consider how people interact with each other in an informal setting when a performance of music is involved. To do this, use or imagination or, perhaps, host a "salon" of your own, with some of your friends invited for an hour or two to listen to music and maybe have a snack. Consider how the interests and personalities of the people affect the surroundings or the choice of music. Is it difficult "just" to listen to music without watching something or entertaining yourself in another way? How do you think the way you and your friends react is similar to, or different from, guests at an aristocratic salon in the early 19th century?

4. During the Schumanns' concert tour to Russia in 1844, one of the guests at a reception honoring Clara tried to make polite conversation with Robert by asking him, "Are you musical as well?" Based on what you can learn about Clara and Robert, if you had been a close friend of the couple, what would have been your response to this question? Continue deeper into the story of the Schumann's marriage and life together and highlight the strongest points in their musical and personal relationship.

VIEWING GUIDE

1. The _____ was the most popular stringed instrument during the "Elizabethan" era. The Elizabethan Era was named for _____ _____ who died in _____. The major author of that period was _____ and arguably the most popular songwriter was named _____.

2. According to Bob Falls, founder of *Poetry Alive!*, a simple definition of poetry would be _____ _____.

3. Three requirements for optimal performance of a "good" song: _____ _____ _____ _____.

4. Most songs benefit from a _____ (size) environment.

5. Poetry can be performed in two ways: _____ or _____.

6. List a few of the topics that were popular in poetry and song in the 19th century: _____ _____

_____.

7. During the 19th century, a *salon* was _____
_____
_____.

8. These qualities are necessary to call a poem a ballad: _____
_____
_____
_____.

9. *In media res* means _____.

10. In Goethe's ballad *Erlkönig*, the singer must convey the _____ (how many?) different characters in the story: (name them) _____
_____
_____.

11. The song cycle, or *Liederkreis*, was "invented" during the (when?) ___
_____.

12. Schumann was drawn to Heine's *Dichterliebe* in part because _____
_____
_____.

13. The first song of the cycle *Dichterliebe* is called "Im wunderschönen Monat Mai" and it is quite a happy song. This is noteworthy because _____
_____
_____.

14. There are moments of irony in this song cycle, including when the singer sings "Ich grolle nicht," which means _____. But the composer (ironically) sets the words into music (how?) _____
_____
_____.

15. The final song, and the entire cycle, ends with _____
_____.

Unit 11 Timeline

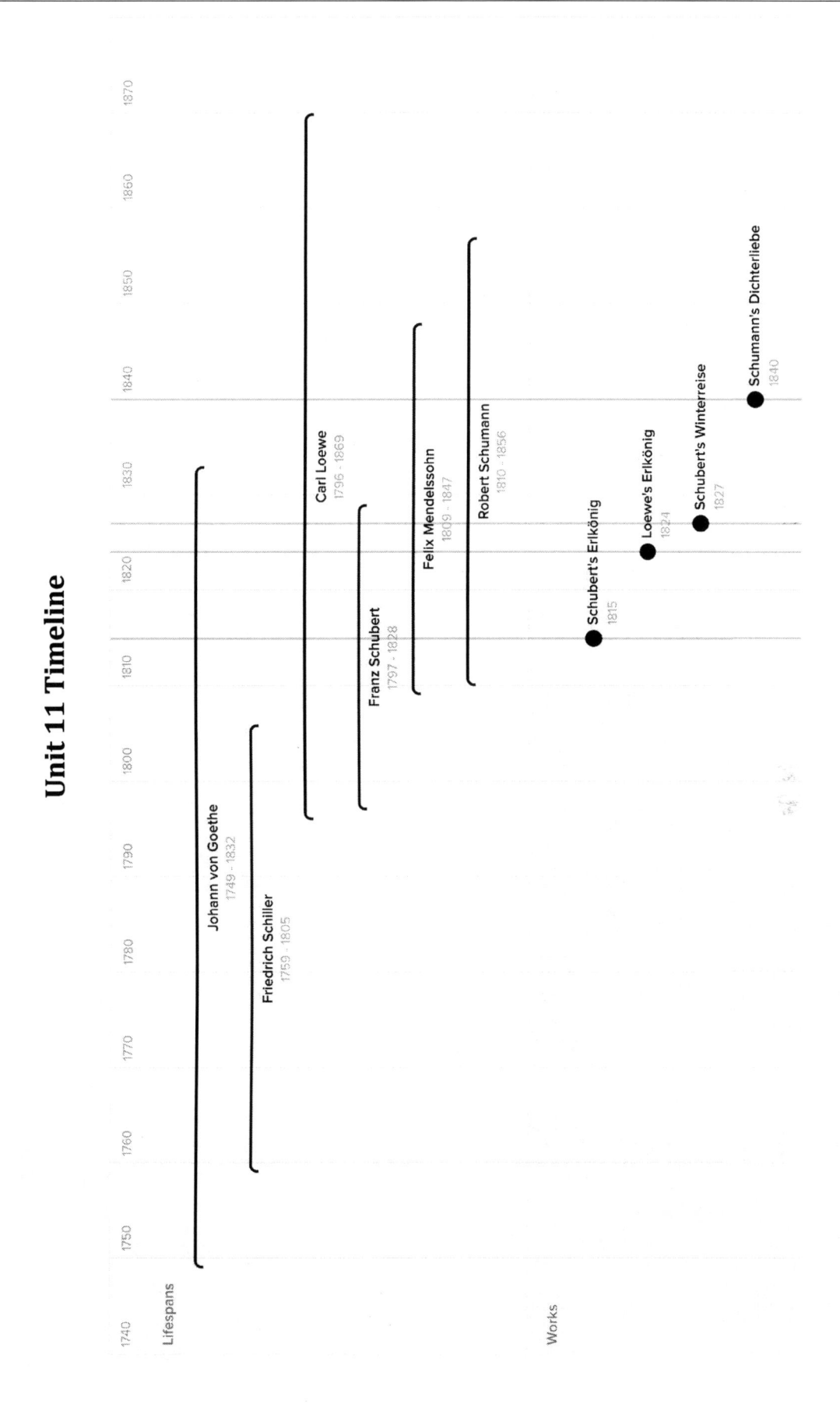

Lifespans

- Johann von Goethe, 1749 - 1832
- Friedrich Schiller, 1759 - 1805
- Franz Schubert, 1797 - 1828
- Carl Loewe, 1796 - 1869
- Felix Mendelssohn, 1809 - 1847
- Robert Schumann, 1810 - 1856

Works

- Schubert's Erlkönig, 1815
- Loewe's Erlkönig, 1824
- Schubert's Winterreise, 1827
- Schumann's Dichterliebe, 1840

124 DISCOVERING MUSIC STUDENT WORKBOOK

Dates ⟶

Unit 12

A Tale of Four Virtuosi and the Birth of the Tone Poem

PEOPLE

Paganini
Nicolò

1782-1840
Romantic

Italy
Violinist, Composer

Chopin
Frédéric

1810-1849
Romantic

Poland, France
Composer

Liszt
Franz

1811-1886
Romantic

Hungary, Germany
Composer

Mendelssohn
Felix

1809-1847
Romantic

Germany
Composer

Mendelssohn
Moses

1729-1786
Classical

Germany
Philospher

Hensel
Fanny Mendelssohn

1805-1847
Romantic

Germany
Composer

Sand
George (Aurore Dudevant)

1804-1876
Romantic

France
Writer

Berlioz
Hector

1803-1869
Romantic

France
Composer

Field
John

1782-1837
Romantic

Ireland
Composer

PLACES

Genoa, Italy	44°24'20.34" N 8°56'46.52" E
Venice, Italy	45°26'02.80" N 12°20'20.47" E
Paris, France	48°51'23.81" N 2°21'08.00" E
Budapest, Hungary	47°29'52.48" N 19°02'24.85" E
Raiding, Hungary	47°35'55.09" N 16°31'51.87" E
Weimar, Germany	
Goethe's House	50°58'39.70" N 11°19'42.97" E
National Theater	50°58'47.39" N 11°19'33.29" E
Altenburg	50°58'57.28" N 11°20'07.24" E
Liszt Garden House	50°58'29.55" N 11°19'48.06" E
Mendelssohn House, Leipzig	51°20'10.53" N 12°22'59.80" E
Warsaw, Poland	52°13'46.83" N 21°00'44.02" E

VOCABULARY

Etude
From *étudier*, the French verb meaning "to study." Within a musical context, an etude is a composition designed to exercise the player's ability to perform a certain skill or technical challenge on an instrument. Usually, etudes utilize that technical challenge in much more difficult and exhausting ways than in ordinary pieces. Therefore, someone who can play the etude is better equipped to execute any ordinary piece successfully.

Character Piece
This is a very general category that includes all kinds of "little" instrumental pieces, especially those that became popular during the 19th century. Chopin and his contemporaries, especially, composed literally hundreds of them for the piano. "Character Pieces" include the

> **Berceuse**, or lullaby
> **Nocturne**, or night piece
> **Barcarolle**, or boating song
> **Prelude**, which is often not a "prelude to" anything
> **Ballade**, or narrative style, free-form piece with a direct opening
> **Rhapsody**, or free-form emotional piece
> **Intermezzo**, which gives the impression of being an interlude, or connecting two larger works

Polonaise
Originally an old style of Polish national dance, the Polonaises written by Chopin became grand, virtuosic pieces for the piano.

Tone Poem (Symphonic Poem)
A composition for instruments, usually an orchestra or wind band, that seeks to describe a central theme, story, or emotion, using the language of music. Tone poems have titles and even "programs" or specific predetermined outlines that give the details of the music's contents. Tone poems often rely upon *leading* or *guiding* motives (leitmotifs or *Leitmotiven*) to keep momentum going and to give a structure to the piece. Hector Berlioz is credited for the first tone poem, with his *Symphonie fantastique* in 1830, but Franz Liszt developed the idea methodically and richly, especially while living in Weimar from 1848 until 1861. He preferred to call his creations "Symphonic Poems." In the 19th century, tone poems were viewed as threatening to traditional symphonies and well-established musical forms. The debate over the tone poem was a large part of the "War of the Romantics."

Gewandhaus (*Gewand* = garment) + (*Haus* = house)
This world-famous concert hall in Leipzig has been home to the celebrated Gewandhaus Orchestra for more than two centuries. The building was originally the home to Leipzig's fabric guild until a group of Leipzig merchants founded a concert society and appropriated the hall for its use. It was the home to many celebrated artistic directors, including Felix Mendelssohn.

DATES

1825	Opening of the Erie Canal
1829	Mendelssohn conducts a revival of J.S. Bach's *St. Matthew Passion*.
1830	Berlioz composes his *Symphonie fantastique*.
1830-1831	Revolution in Poland
1831	Liszt hears Paganini perform.
	Cyrus McCormick invents the first commercial reaper.
1834	Slavery abolished throughout the British Empire.
1835	Mendelssohn appointed conductor at the Leipzig Gewandhaus.
1836	Battle of the Alamo
1837	Samuel Morse invents the Telegraph.
1837-1901	Queen Victoria rules the British Empire, the "Victorian" Era.
1840	Friedrich Wilhelm IV crowned King of Prussia.

LISTENING

See Listening Guide at http://www.professorcarol.com/dm-listening

Most of the selections for this unit are relatively short, in keeping with the nature of the "character piece" and music for the salon. But the varieties of virtuosity require multiple examples.

PUTTING IT ALL TOGETHER

1. In this unit, we have introduced you to some of "classical" music's most colorful celebrities—the virtuosi who captured the imagination of audiences in the 19th century. Because these composers lived and performed as famous individuals, we have much information available to tell us where and when they performed, what kinds of things they thought were important, what kind of friends they had, and what kinds of lives they led. Spend some time researching in more depth the life and compositions of one or more of the composers discussed in this unit. You may want to spend just enough time to get acquainted with each one, or you may already have a favorite on whom you want to focus. Be able to answer some of the following questions:

- What was this composer best known for in his or her lifetime: performing or composing?
- What other famous friends did this person have?
- What important people did this person meet or play for?
- Did this person have other famous family members?
- Did this person play other instruments?
- What other interests did this person have?
- What was his or her upbringing like? How well educated was this person?
- What authors were important to the composer?
- Was this person wealthy?
- What things about the person's life surprise you?
- At what age did this person die, and what was the cause?
- What past composers did this person try to emulate?

2. Throughout this course, we have focused on the three main sources of support for the arts: the church, royal courts, and the theater. Until the time of Beethoven, composers had to have some kind of job in one of these three places (and maybe more than one!) to survive. How did the virtuosi discussed in this chapter earn their livings? How, or with what, were they paid? How do you think the system for virtuoso performers has changed? How do they launch careers today? Where do they perform? How are they paid? How is their fame promoted?

3. Research the tone (symphonic) poems of Liszt. What do you learn about this genre? Upon what are tone poems usually based? Without words, how do they tell their stories? Research the story behind one of Liszt's tone poems and listen to at least one performance.

4. In this unit, the Mendelssohn family is unique because of the number of famous members who are discussed. Research the three members of the Mendelssohn family. For what accomplishments was Moses Mendelssohn most famous? What was the profession of Fanny's husband? What can you learn about Mendelssohn's wife Cecile?

5. Today, we have a very clear idea of what a "concert" should be. What are some of the (many) differences you can think of between a contemporary concert today and concerts during the early 19th century? What would be fun about attending a concert back in Liszt's or Paganini's day?

6. One kind of concert today is called a recital: this is essentially a concert where usually one or two players perform as soloists and receive all of the focus. Do some research and find a recital in your area: even if you cannot purchase tickets to hear the performance of someone well known or a recital in a fancy hall, you might be able to find recitals in the following locations. Many will be very inexpensive, or even free!

- Churches
- Community and senior centers (check your local newspaper)
- Libraries
- Local universities or colleges
- Museums
- Cultural centers

Whether or not you can attend such a performance, try to learn what pieces will be played. Describe what you think will be the environment and general feeling of the event. Also, develop a habit of regularly checking for performances in these locations. You may be surprised at what interesting concerts, recitals, and performance events take place!

7. You may also wish to look at the concert and recital listings in a big metropolitan area (via newspapers or online). Check Chicago, New York, Los Angeles, Dallas, or Boston, for example. Figure out what is being performed when, and in what kind of hall. Try to find out who the "star" players are and what music they are performing. Which performances would you like to attend? What would the tickets cost? If possible, follow up after the concert(s) by reading reviews published in a newspaper or online.

Unit 12: A Tale of Four Virtuosi and the Birth of the Tone Poem

VIEWING GUIDE

1. What do you think draws audiences to virtuoso musicians? _____ _____

2. The first superstar virtuoso of the Romantic period was _____ _____.

3. What things about Paganini helped to make him famous? _____ _____ _____.

4. The Romantic ideal considered art and artistic creativity to be _____ _____ _____.

5. The young Paganini practiced his violin up to _____ hours per day!

6. Another virtuoso who emulated Paganini was the pianist _____ _____.

7. Unlike Paganini, Liszt _____ _____.

8. Liszt spent many grueling (if sometimes glamorous) years on stage as a _____ and he went virtually all over _____ _____.

9. While in Paris, Liszt's friends included _____, _____, and _____.

10. During this time, what nickname did Paris gain? _____ _____. What had the Baroque King Louis XIV done to contribute to this nickname? _____ _____.

11. After Liszt left the stage, he went to _____ in order to ___ _____. Later, he moved to _____ so that he could _____.

12. P.T. Barnum filled his circus acts with many "wonders of the world," including (from music) _____ such as the famous singer _____ from (country) _____.

13. Name some ways Chopin's music was different from that of Liszt or

Paganini. _____
_____
_____.

14. The French verb *étudier* means _____. An étude is ____
_____.

15. Though he was _____ (nationality), Chopin left his home at a young age to move to a very exciting Western European city, namely _____.

16. Did he ever move back home? Yes ____ No ____

17. What is a "character piece"? _____
_____.

18. Though Chopin is famous for his nocturnes, this kind of piece is said to have been invented by an _____ (nationality) composer and pianist named _____.

19. Chopin is famous for his piano pieces. What kinds of works expected of a 19th-century composer did he *not* compose? _____
_____
_____.

20. Although Felix Mendelssohn's family eventually became Protestant (Lutheran), his ethnicity was _____.

21. Mendelssohn composed oratorios on what two famous Biblical stories? _____ and _____.

22. Mendelssohn was also a principal figure in reviving interest in the compositions of one of our mega-composers, namely _____.

23. Mendelssohn was also an accomplished _____, who recorded many scenes from his travels to Italy and Switzerland.

24. Mendelssohn had a close relationship with his sister _____, _____, also an accomplished pianist and composer.

25. Mendelssohn was one of the first persons to raise the standards for _____ (musical position).

26. Concerts in the early 19th century usually included _____
_____

Unit 12: A Tale of Four Virtuosi and the Birth of the Tone Poem   133

_____.

27. What are "Symphonic Poems" (Tone Poems)? _____
_____
_____.

28. Who composed the *Symphonie fantastique*? _____. What inspired the work? _____
_____.

29. Liszt's followers called themselves the "Altenburg Eagles." What was the "Altenburg"? _____
_____.

30. As *Kapellmeister* in Weimar, Liszt was in a situation where _____
_____
_____.

31. The troublesome German genius-composer whose music Liszt championed was named _____.

134 DISCOVERING MUSIC STUDENT WORKBOOK

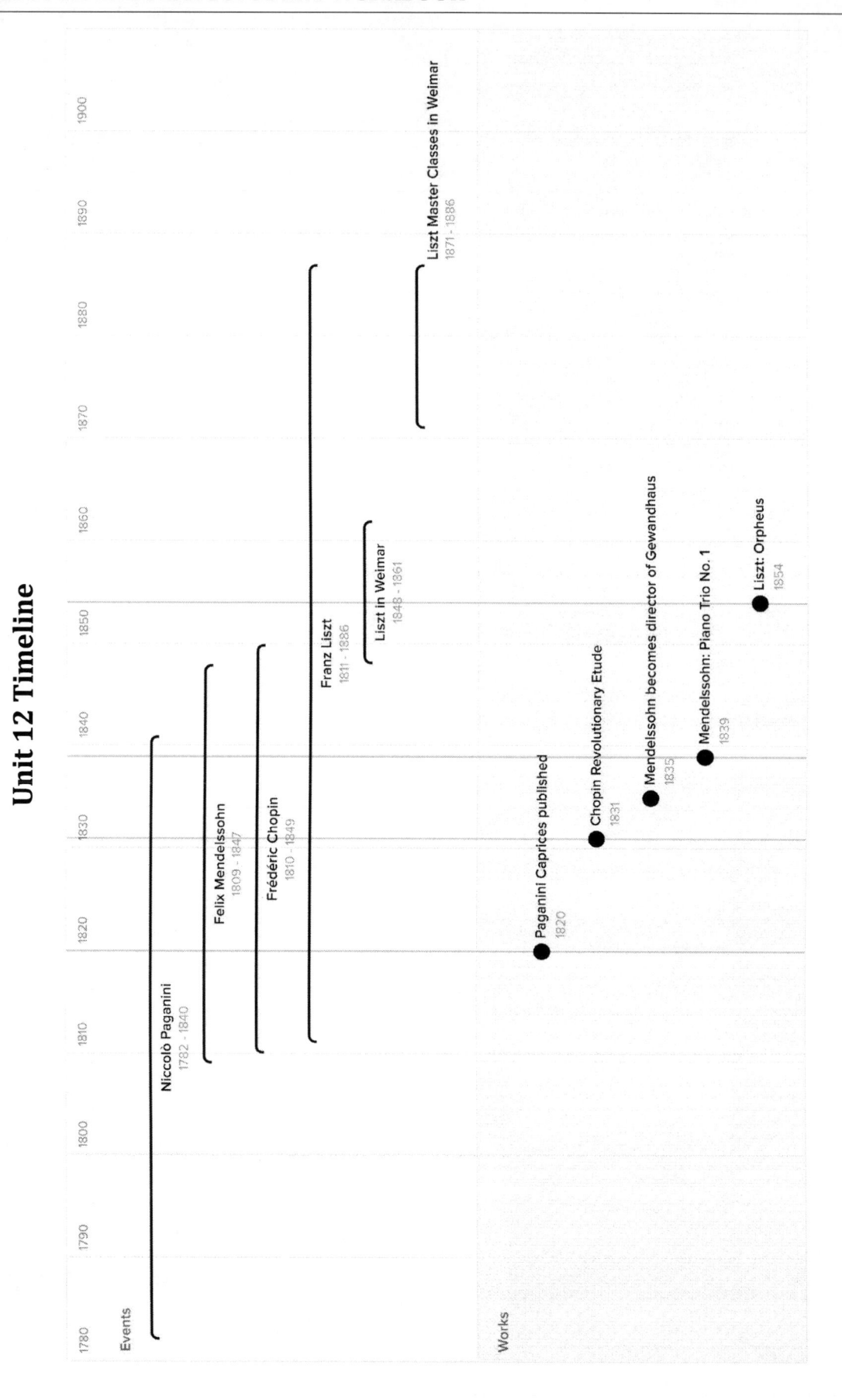

Unit 12 Timeline

Events

- Niccolò Paganini, 1782 - 1840
- Felix Mendelssohn, 1809 - 1847
- Frédéric Chopin, 1810 - 1849
- Franz Liszt, 1811 - 1886
- Liszt in Weimar, 1848 - 1861
- Liszt Master Classes in Weimar, 1871 - 1886

Works

- Paganini Caprices published, 1820
- Chopin Revolutionary Etude, 1831
- Mendelssohn becomes director of Gewandhaus, 1835
- Mendelssohn: Piano Trio No. 1, 1839
- Liszt: Orpheus, 1854

Unit 12: A Tale of Four Virtuosi and the Birth of the Tone Poem   135

YOUR TIMELINE

Dates ⟶

Unit 13

Nationalism and the Explosion of Romantic Opera

PEOPLE

Rossini
Gioachino

1792-1868
Romantic

Italy
Composer

Bellini
Vincenzo

1801-1835
Romantic

Italy
Composer

Donizetti
Gaetano

1797-1848
Romantic

Italy
Composer

Meyerbeer
Giacomo

1791-1864
Romantic

Germany
Composer

Weber
Carl Maria

1786-1826
Romantic

Germany
Composer

Bizet
Georges

1838-1875
Romantic

France
Composer

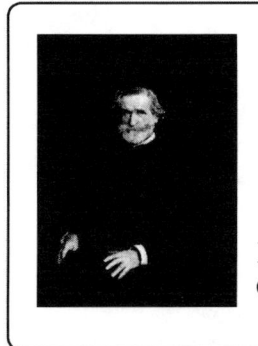

Verdi
Giuseppi
1813-1901
Romantic

Italy
Composer

Puccini
Giacomo
1858-1924
Romantic

Italy
Composer

Scott
Walter
1771-1832
Romantic

Scotland
Writer

Adam
Adolphe
1803-1856
Romantic

French
Composer

PLACES

Each "Place" in this unit is home to a famous opera house.

Paris, Place de l'Opéra	48°52'14.29" N 2°19'55.51" E
Venice, Teatro La Fenice	45°26'01.10" N 12°20'01.53" E
Dresden Oper	51°03'19.87" N 13°44'07.95" E
Hamburg Staatsoper	53°33'23.51" N 9°59'25.36" E
Milan La Scala	45°28'02.47" N 9°11'22.81" E
Prague National Theater	50°04'51.61" N 14°24'48.86" E
Prague Estates Theater	50°05'09.52" N 14°25'25.19" E
Vienna State Opera	48°12'11.50" N 16°22'10.95" E
Sydney Opera House	33°51'24.45" S 151°12'55.07" E

VOCABULARY

Minuet

An early type of social dance (particularly popular in the 18th century) requiring the dancing couple to make specific physical (palm-to-palm) contact with one another. It has a triple meter, i.e. three beats per measure: 1-2-3, 1-2-3. Eventually, minuets became so popular that many composers wrote pieces in the style of a minuet just for listening rather than for dancing. Minuets often were structured with a contrasting middle section (called a Trio) that had a thinner texture, after which the first section would be repeated. So we talk about a "minuet and trio" form, or A-B-A.

Waltz

A later social dance that became popular in the late 18th century. It dominated the mid and late 19th century. The waltz was characterized by a triple meter and a robust tempo. The waltz rhythm found its way into many pieces of music in the 19th century, from operas to symphonies. Waltzing required more physical contact than the minuet, and was considered scandalous by some. Its energetic steps required the man to encircle the woman's waist, and the woman to hold onto his shoulder. Because of the spinning, the dancers had to lock eyes in order not to become dizzy. This was considered "dangerous" in an era when extreme public modesty was the rule.

Ballet

From the Italian verb *ballare*, which means "to dance." By the 19th century, ballet had become a highly disciplined style of formal dancing intended for staged performance. Unlike folk dancing, it had to be seriously studied from a young age to be mastered. Although most ballet evenings consist now solely of dances, ballets first appeared as *intermezzi* between the acts of an opera or play. Ballet grew from court dancing (see Unit 4 and Louis XIV). The biggest innovation in the 19th century was dancing on the toe (for women), or *en pointe*, developed about 1830. Ballet in the 1830s and 1840s goes by the name Romantic Ballet. After the middle of the 19th century, an even more elaborate vocabulary of *en pointe* dancing became known as Classical Ballet.

Singspiel (*singen* = to sing) + (*spielen* = to play)

Singspiel is a form of dialogue opera in which the arias (songs) are sung, while the information and dialogue (or conversation) is spoken. Unlike Italian opera, in which all of the story is sung throughout, whether in recitative or aria, the Germans initially found that their language worked best in opera if the dialogue were set in normal speech and the emotional parts (arias) were sung. So too did the English and a few other national groups.

French Grand Opera

This style of opera was uniquely French in its grandeur. French "grand" operas were epic performances usually based upon sweeping and complex historical subjects. They generally had five acts and tackled serious historical topics. They included at least one ballet (dance episode) and had big scenes for chorus. As a result, these beautiful and fascinating productions were (and are) incredibly expensive—one main reason these works are performed less often. An example of French Grand Opera would be Meyerbeer's *Les Huguenots*.

Bel canto (*bel* = beautiful) + (*canto* = singing)
Although all opera is intended to be "sung beautifully," *bel canto* describes a specific kind of singing vocal technique going all the way back to the 1600s. The term also refers to a type of operatic role in the 1700s and 1800s that emphasizes expression of the voice and ornate vocal melodies. *Bel canto* opera relies on virtuosic singing (coloratura) in the high register (soprano/tenor) plus a direct emotional appeal of the story, rather than "grand" costumes, elaborate decorations, or historical weight. *Bel canto* opera can be serious or comic. An example of a comic *bel canto* opera would be Rossini's *Barber of Seville*, while a tragic one would be Bellini's *Norma*.

Risorgimento
Il Risorgimento (Italian for the Resurgence) was the socio-political movement that led to the unification of the independent Italian states into one united nation called Italy. This long-overdue movement began during the end of Napoleon's rule and led to the establishment of the Kingdom of Italy 1861. It is, however, common to speak about Italian music or Italian literature long before there was a country called "Italy."

Verismo
A "realistic" approach to theater, including opera. *Verismo* opera is usually dark and tragic. Although not the earliest, the composer Puccini is most often credited with writing the finest *verismo* operas (*Tosca* and *Madame Butterfly*). Decades earlier, Verdi was incorporating quite a bit of realism into his operas with tragic endings (*La Traviata*). Certain other tragic operas are famous particularly for their *verismo* intensity (*I Pagliacci* by Leoncavallo and *Cavalleria Rusticanna* by Mascagni). The popularity of *verismo* will be a step along the way to an emotionally searing early 20th-century artistic movement called Expressionism (Unit 17).

DATES

1815-1871	Italian *Risorgimento*
1821	Weber's *Der Freischütz* has its premiere.
1831	*En pointe* dancing steals the show in Meyerbeer's *Robert le Diable*.
1852	Harriet Beecher Stowe publishes *Uncle Tom's Cabin*.
1853	*La Traviata* has its premier in Venice.
1854	Crimean War
	Kansas-Nebraska Act
1860	South Carolina becomes first state to secede from the Union.

1861	Unified Kingdom of Italy established
	Serfdom abolished in Russia.
1861-1865	The American Civil War
1870-1871	The Franco-Prussian War
1871	Germany is unified as one nation.
	The Suez Canal is completed.
	Verdi's *Aida* is premiered in Cairo, Egypt.
1876	Invention of the telephone
	Battle of Little Bighorn
	First performance of Wagner's *Ring* in the *Festspielhaus* [see Unit 14]
1877	Invention of Edison's gramophone

LISTENING

See Listening Guide at http://www.professorcarol.com/dm-listening

Listening selections provide examples of bel canto and verismo.

RECOMMENDED FOR INTRODUCING OPERAS AND BALLETS

Puccini - *Turandot at the Forbidden City of Beijing*, conducted by Zubin Mehta. Maggio Musicale Fiorentino (1998)
A remarkable documentary, this DVD shows the construction of a production of *Turandot* at the great opera house of La Scala in Italy. The production then was taken to the Forbidden City in China. A splendid way for the whole family to see how an opera is produced and to marvel at the resources China contributed to the production. The costumes and sets are blindingly beautiful. And there are interviews with the singers, directors, even officials involved in the delicate matter of transporting an Italian theatrical production to China.

Verdi. *Otello*. Directed by Franco Zefferelli. Teatro la Scala. Plácido Domingo and Katia Ricciarelli (1986)
This attractive movie version of *Otello* is smartly done with wonderful sets, realistic acting, and the fantastic voices of Placido Domingo and Katia Ricciarelli. In addition to being impressive as a film, it will provide an excellent basis for a comparison with Shakespeare's *Othello*.

Verdi. *La Traviata*. Directed by Franco Zefferelli. The Metropolitan Opera, conducted by James Levine. Plácido Domingo, Theresa Stratas (1983).
This heart-breaker is well done as a movie, with lovely sets. The opera is performed straight through (with subtitles, of course), and its movie-like aspect should capture the attention of those new to opera.

Adam. *Giselle*. Natalia Markarova, Mikhail Baryshnikov, American Ballet Theater (1992)
There are literally dozens of performances of *Giselle* available on DVD. This performance with Baryshnikov and Markarova is a classic, but you should try several productions for comparisons! Try any Russian production, especially the Kirov Ballet (Leningrad/St. Petersburg), or the 2008 production by the National Ballet of Paris and National Orchestra of Paris. There is an older performance that features legendary dancer Rudolph Nureyev, and while the video quality may not be as "modern," the dancing is phenomenal.

Bizet. *Carmen*. Directed by Carlos Saura with Antonio Gades (1983) Flamenco-Film Version.
A fascinating new way to look at *Carmen*, featuring the virtuoso dancing of Antonio Gades. Saura has created a story-within-a-story, in which a group of professional flamenco dancers are preparing a flamenco production of *Carmen*. Suddenly, a Carmen-like situation develops within the company. The principal parts of the opera are all heard, and the flamenco dancing is magnificent. Plus, you'll get an idea of how a dance production is rehearsed. There are gripping scenes, and viewers are likely to be entranced. Also, you can discuss how a story-within-a-story drama works. (There's a long tradition of this dramatic structure—start with a familiar one such as Shakespeare's *Hamlet*.)

PUTTING IT ALL TOGETHER

1. Find a recorded (DVD, VHS) copy of at least one of the operas on your listening list. (You may also find a production online.) It's far better to choose one with subtitles, since knowing what is being said is critical for opera. Before you sit down to watch, spend some time becoming familiar with the libretto and the background of the work and try to answer at least some of the following questions:

    - What is the source of this opera's story? (literature, history, mythology)

    - What are the principal roles or characters? What are their voice types (soprano, mezzo soprano/alto, tenor, baritone, bass)?

    - Into how many acts is the opera divided?

    - What is the basic plot?

- Did the composer write many operas and, if so, is this an early, middle, or late work?

- Who was the librettist? Did the composer often work with the librettist?

- Was this opera well-received, popular?

- If considered "important," then why?

Consider proceeding one act at a time, and then reflecting on it. After you have watched the entire work, think about the production—the way the opera is staged. For example, it is set in what time period (this may be quite different from the original idea of the opera)? What kind of sets and costumes do you see, and do they play a strong role in the production (are they unusual, attention-grabbing)? What is the overall atmosphere of the production? What do you find most engaging about this particular production? What disappoints you?

Make sure to trigger the English subtitles in whatever production you watch or stream.

2. What is the nearest opera company to where you live (in big cities, you may have several)? See if you can answer these questions.

- What is its history (who founded it, when, at what point in the city's development)? What performing facility does it use (beautiful historic theater, new theater built for operas and plays, general-purpose auditorium, church, school auditorium, or other site)?

- Where do the singers and orchestral musicians come from (local, regional, or guest artists from afar)?

- Where do they rehearse?

- How often do they perform?

- What repertoire will they offer in the next season?

- How is the company regarding nationally or internationally?

3. If possible, set up a field trip to view the rehearsal facilities of your local opera. Most companies (even small ones) have a public relations liaison who will be happy to show you around and tell you or your group about their work. See if you can find out the answers to any of these questions:

- How long is the company's "season," and how many productions are performed?

- Who decides which productions to perform?

- What is the budget for the entire season? For each production?

- Do they own the productions, or do they rent them (sets, costumes, etc.)?

- How far in advance do they decide on the productions and book the singers?

- How old is this company? Has it changed over the years?

- What are the present goals of this company?

- What factors (economic, geographic, civic, artistic) are helping to shape the company's future?

If at all possible, attend an actual rehearsal, preferably one where the work really is in preparation, so you can see how the vocal parts are worked out, as well as the blocking and staging.

4. Take time to visit the website of two of the opera houses listed above under "Places." Such wonderful opera houses usually have equally gorgeous websites, so this should be a real pleasure! (If you need a little help with the foreign languages, look for the English translation button as necessary.) For each opera house, try to answer the following:

- In what year was their original theater built?

- Has it ever been destroyed and/or needed to be rebuilt? Remember: some of these buildings have existed through two World Wars, plus at least one national revolution!

- What operas are in their current season (a season runs from fall through spring)?

- Does the website show excerpts and promotions of performances?

- Can you find any "backstage" features or interviews online?

- Does the house offer tours to people visiting the city? (Most big houses do, often in many languages, and they are popular with tourists.)

- How often do they offer performances?

- What is the price range for seating?

- Are tickets generally available or are most productions "sold out" long in advance?

- Does the house offer "standing" places? Standing places are very popular in the famous houses, and long lines of students and tourists almost always form, full of people eager to wait in line for hours just to stand through a full-length opera!

- Does the opera have any corporate sponsors?

144 DISCOVERING MUSIC STUDENT WORKBOOK

VIEWING GUIDE

1. Western ballet goes back to the court of _____. The biggest social-dance craze of the 18th century was the _____. Then, moving into the 19th century, the _____ became popular, and it was more physically intimate and athletic.

2. The word "ballet" comes from the Italian verb *ballare*, meaning _____.

3. About 1800, the German composer _____ wrote the first musical score specifically designed for a ballet.

4. Ballet from the first half of the 19th century is known (stylistically) as _____, while ballet from the second half is known as _____. This is worth noting, because in music, the labels are used differently: the 18th-century style of music called _____ *precedes* the 19th-century style called the _____.

5. Dancing *en pointe* was initially intended to depict _____ _____.

6. The first act of *Giselle* is based on a popular 18th-century style of story known in literature as _____, while the spooky second act reflects the trendy world of the new _____ style. The female spirits wanting to gain revenge in Act II are called the _____.

7. *Giselle* also had a _____ scene where the main character dances herself to death. This kind of scene became popular in the 19th century. There's an especially good one in Donizetti's opera _____ _____, based on a novel by the popular English writer _____ _____.

8. One last point about *Giselle*: Adam uses themes called _____ to signify characters or objects. This technique of matching musical patterns to objects or ideas will become common in later 19th-century music.

9. The _____ (nationality) greatly preferred to have much dancing in their _____ (what kind of entertainment?). They also liked visually extravagant scenes such as _____ _____.

Unit 13: Nationalism and the Explosion of Romantic Opera   145

10. An important theme in 19th-century opera is _____ _____. Another important "spiritual" theme, particularly in German opera, is _____.

11. German opera was changed forever in _____ (date) with a *Singspiel* called *Der Freischütz*, or "The Free Shot." This opera was especially popular with German audiences because _____ _____ _____.

12. Germany did not become a united country until after the _____ _____ in _____ (date). Italy did not become united as a country until _____ (date).

13. In America, we also like the *Singspiel* format, but we don't usually call it "opera." Rather, we call it a _____.

14. What is the difference between an "ordinary" opera and a *Singspiel*, or "dialogue" opera? _____ _____.

15. Do 19th-century operas depend upon a *lieto fine*? _____ _____.

16. Who were the three greatest Italian opera composers in the first half of the 19th century (their names end in "i")? _____ _____ _____.

17. *Bel canto* means literally _____.

18. Rossini excelled at many things, including writing excellent opening numbers called _____ and weaving the music and action of several characters together, in what we call _____.

19. Verdi's opera *Nabucco* tells the Biblical story of King _____ _____. The famous chorus called _____ is familiar to nearly every Italian, even today.

20. What is a *scena ed aria*? _____ _____.

21. What was the *Risorgimento*? _____ _____

146 DISCOVERING MUSIC STUDENT WORKBOOK

22. *Viva Verdi* became a code for what revolutionary cry? _____. Why was it necessary to use this seemingly innocent phrase as a political code? _____ _____.

23. What culture seemed especially exotic to the French? _____.

24. Bizet's opera *Carmen* broke new ground because of the way it ended, namely _____. That kind of "realism" has a name in theater: _____.

25. Radio broadcasts of _____, sponsored for decades by _____, were long a great source for listening to opera for people living outside of New York City or other big cities.

Unit 13 Timeline

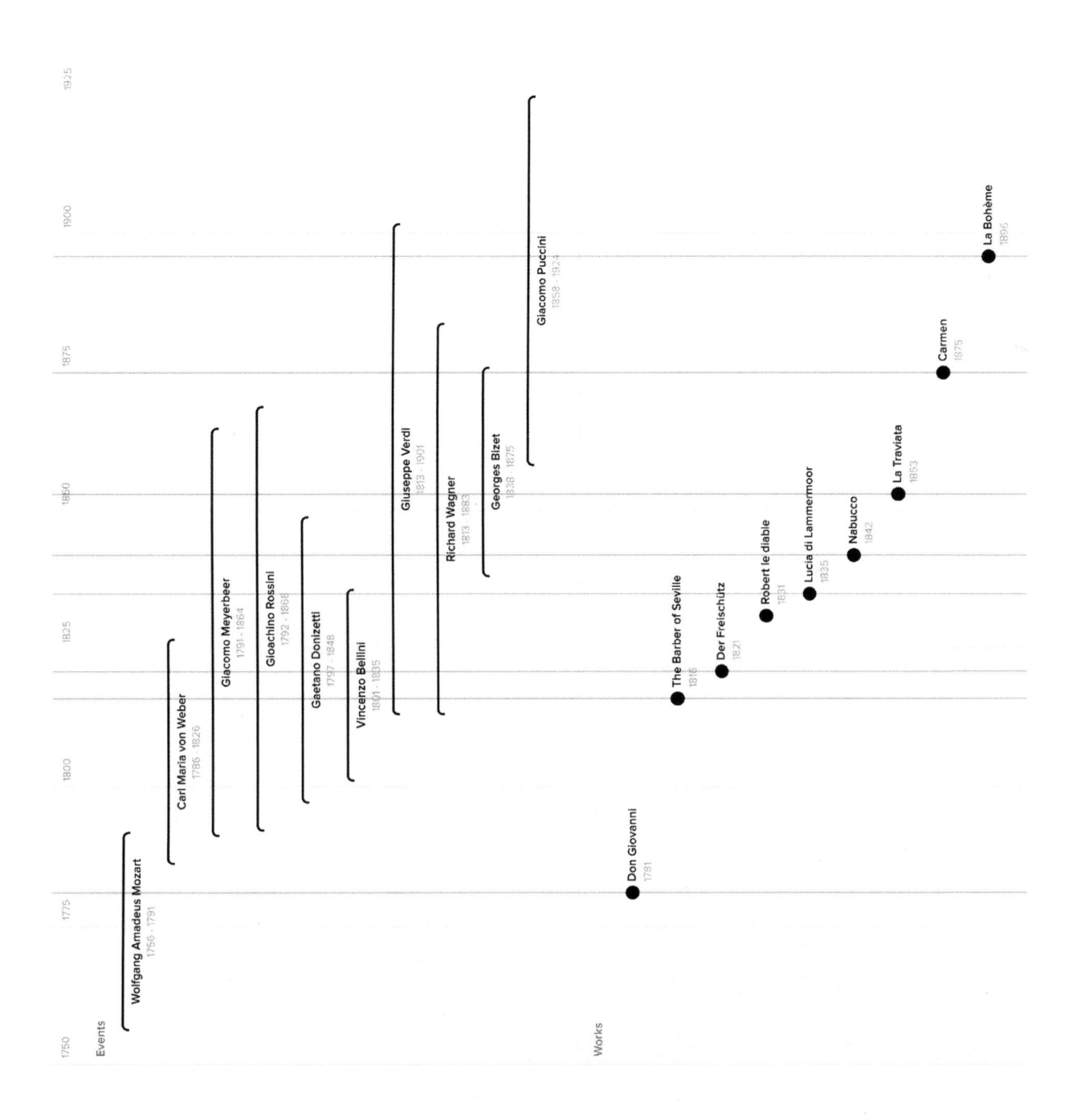

Events

- Wolfgang Amadeus Mozart (1756–1791)
- Carl Maria von Weber (1786–1826)
- Giacomo Meyerbeer (1791–1864)
- Gioachino Rossini (1792–1868)
- Gaetano Donizetti (1797–1848)
- Vincenzo Bellini (1801–1835)
- Giuseppe Verdi (1813–1901)
- Richard Wagner (1813–1883)
- Georges Bizet (1838–1875)
- Giacomo Puccini (1858–1924)

Works

- Don Giovanni — 1787
- The Barber of Seville — 1816
- Der Freischütz — 1821
- Robert le diable — 1831
- Lucia di Lammermoor — 1835
- Nabucco — 1842
- La Traviata — 1853
- Carmen — 1875
- La Bohème — 1896

148 DISCOVERING MUSIC STUDENT WORKBOOK

YOUR TIMELINE

Dates ⟶

Unit 14

The Absolutely New World of Wagner

PEOPLE

Wagner
Richard
1813-1883
Romantic

Germany
Composer

Ludwig II
1845-1886
Romantic

Bavaria
King

Liszt
Franz
1811-1886
Romantic

Hungary, Germany
Composer

PLACES

Festspielhaus, Bayreuth	49°57'35.48" N 11°34'47.07" E
Wahnfried, Bayreuth	49°56'27.48" N 11°34'55.51" E
Wartburg Castle	50°57'58.83" N 10°18'22.83" E
Riga, Latvia	56°56'58.73" N 24°06'18.67" E
Weimar	50°58'47.39" N 11°19'33.29" E
Dresden	51°03'19.87" N 13°44'07.95" E
Paris	48°52'14.29" N 2°19'55.51" E

VOCABULARY

Gesamtkunstwerk (*gesamt* = collected, participle from *sammeln* = to collect) + (*Kunst* = art) + (*Werk* = work)
"Total" or "Complete" art work; this term sums up Wagner's philosophy of how artistic productions should be conceived by the creator and consumed by the audience.

Das Kunstwerk der Zukunft (*Kunstwerk* = artwork) + (*der* = of the) + (*Zukunft* = future)
Artwork of the Future" (1849); the essay in which Wagner explains the idea of fusing music with staged drama, justifying his ideas by linking them to a legendary German past.

Leitmotiv (*leiten* = to guide, lead) + (*Motiv* = motive)
Guiding motives, used throughout Wagner's works to guide or lead the listener through his complex compositions; they can roughly be thought of as "theme music" or "signature tunes" not only for characters but for characteristic ideas, places, and concepts in the Ring cycle.

Festspielhaus (*Fest* = festival) + (*Spiel* = play) + (*Haus* = house)
The opera house designed by Wagner specifically for the performance of his works, especially the Ring cycle. Located in Bayreuth, in Bavaria (southern part of Germany), the *Festspielhaus* includes a number of structural and design elements that were revolutionary during Wagner's time; today most have become common elements of performance spaces.

Courtly Love
The medieval ideal of relationships between men and women in which a man (a knight) sought the attention and support of his lady (typically a noblewoman). The legend of King Arthur and Guinevere is one example.

Meistersinger
A member of a German guild of poetry and art song in the 14th, 15th, and 16th centuries that followed and preserved the traditions of the Minnesingers.

Minnesinger
The *Minnesinger* (plural *Minnesänger*) was a 12th- to 13th-century German poet-musician who crafted songs about the joys and follies of courtly love.

Novella
A fictional literary work, designated by its length; it is shorter than a full-length novel, but longer than most short stories. A *musical novella* may feature a musician as a principal character or use the power of music as a force in the plot.

Nibelungenlied
"Song of the Nibelung"; this epic poem, used by Wagner as part of the inspiration for the libretto of his Ring Cycle, dates from the early 13th century. Researchers have shown how Wagner wove the *Nibelungenlied* into other, even older, non-German legends to create the

full libretto for his massive operatic tetralogy.

National Socialism (*Nazionalsozialismus*)
Commonly known today as Nazism, this extreme political and social movement is sometimes described as Fascism and was built around scientific theories of racism and anti-semitism. With roots in many eras of Western history, National Socialism arose strongly in 19th-century German thought and was championed by Adolf Hitler.

Wagnerian (adj.)/ Wagneriana (noun, compare with "Beethoveniana")
General terms describing information pertaining to Wagner. These can include anything from the substantial (such as lists of his works) to the trivial (anecdotes related to his descendents or family history). A "Wagnerian" is a person who *loves* Wagner's music.

DATES

1849	Wagner flees Dresden due to anti-government activity. *Das Kunstwerk der Zukunft* is published.
	Gold fever sweeps the United States.
1854	The Kansas-Nebraska Act sparks a bitter controversy between "slave" and "free" states, resulting in open hostilities that would lead to civil war.
1861	Wagner returns to Germany, protected by King Ludwig II.
	Russian serfs are set free by decree under Tsar Alexander II.
1861-1865	American Civil War
1862	Homestead Act is passed in the U.S., beginning the great migration west.
1870-1871	Franco-Prussian War
1876	First full performance of *The Ring* at the opening of the Bayreuth *Festspielhaus*

LISTENING

See Listening Guide at http://www.professorcarol.com/dm-listening

Opera needs to be experienced live. Trying to discover opera by listening to selected brief excerpts is far from ideal. Building a relationship with opera is very much like cultivating a connection with a sport. A clip can't convey the substance, especially when it comes to Wagner's massive operas. There are hours of music from which to choose, but by now you have a sense of how Wagner would have felt about "only" listening to his music, without the experience of the theater and the scenery and the visual elements. Below are listed overtures and sections of Wagner's operas that have become popular in their own right; from there, feel free to venture out on your own!

- "*Beglückt darf nun dich*," the "Pilgrims' Chorus" from *Tannhäuser*, Act III
- Prelude to Act I of *Lohengrin* (1850)
- "*Treulich gefuhrt ziehet dahin*," the "Bridal Chorus" (Wedding March) from *Lohengrin*, Act III
- "Ride of the Valkyries" from *Die Walküre* (*The Valkyries*) (1870)
- Overture to *Die Meistersinger von Nürnberg* (*The Mastersingers of Nuremberg*) (1868)

PUTTING IT ALL TOGETHER

1. There are many epic stories still popular today: Tolkien's *Lord of the Rings* trilogy, Lewis' *Chronicles of Narnia*, and even *Star Wars*, to name just three. What makes a book or movie "epic"? Are you familiar with any literary epics (those listed above, or others)? What are the characteristics of a good epic? What makes an epic compelling? How is the experience different than reading a single, good novel?

2. Choose one of your own favorite movies (one that you know has a strong musical score, such as one with music by John Williams or virtually any of the films of Hollywood's Golden Age in the 1940s and 50s). Pay close attention to how the music relates to the story. Are there specific melodies that seem to match certain characters? How does the soundtrack of the movie make dramatic, sad, or scary parts even more dramatic, sad, or scary? Take two favorite themes and re-watch scenes where they appear after turning down the sound. How does the silence affect the action? If someone were new to this film, and the music was missing (here, or throughout the film), what would change about the viewer's experience?

3. If you have never read the legend of King Arthur, find and read a literary version that is appropriate for you. You may be surprised to find a number of familiar story-telling elements—after all, they've been around a long time! After you finish, make a list of what, to you, were the primary elements of the story (you can start with the sword!).

4. Do some research on the Bayreuth *Festspielhaus*. Review its history. Although built in the 19th century, what about its architectural and design elements seem modern to you. Who sings at the Festspielhaus nowadays? What works are in the current season, or the upcoming season? When are performances held? How much do tickets cost? How would you obtain tickets? Are there other events held during the season, including festivities, meals, or lectures?

Unit 14: The Absolutely New World of Wagner

VIEWING GUIDE

1. The action in Wagner's *The Ring of the Nibelungs* is centered around the _____. These four operas are based on stories from _____ legends.

2. Wagner's family background would be best described as _____.

3. True or False: Hitler and Wagner were close, personal friends. _____

4. Wagner became the musical "poster boy" for National Socialism because _____.

5. Wagner's first fully successful opera, _____, was inspired, in part, by a real scare he had at sea when _____.

6. Wagner's experiences trying to "make it" in Paris were _____.

7. The _____ is the same castle where Martin Luther hid out in _____ (year) in order to _____, and where the legendary character Tannhäuser, centuries earlier, _____.

8. Wagner came up with the term _____ to describe a work that incorporated all of the arts, with a single creator having complete artistic control.

9. In exile, Wagner existed mostly on financial support from _____ (person), who did everything he could to keep people aware of Wagner's music. Later, Wagner was financed by _____ who took the money from Bavaria's state budget!

10. Perhaps Wagner's most famous idea was using a set of pitches called the _____ to represent the different _____ in his complicated opera plots.

11. In Wagner's *Festspielhaus*, the orchestra pit is located largely _____ the stage. Wagner designed it this way so that _____. Wagner even designed a new type of instrument, which we today call the _____

_____.

12. True or False: Wagner wanted people in his audience to relax, socialize, and simply enjoy themselves and have a good time. _____

13. The complete *Ring* lasts approximately _____ hours! It (circle one) was/was not intended to be seen in one long stretch.

14. The Prelude (Wagner's name for Overture) to _____ opens with a long, sustained E-flat chord. Wagner would not have liked us to hear short excerpts from his operas because _____
_____.

15. True or False: There are still people today who would link Wagner to Hitler and National Socialism (Fascism in the 1930s). _____

16. True or False: The Wagner Festival at Bayreuth is a high-profile event still today. _____

Unit 14 Timeline

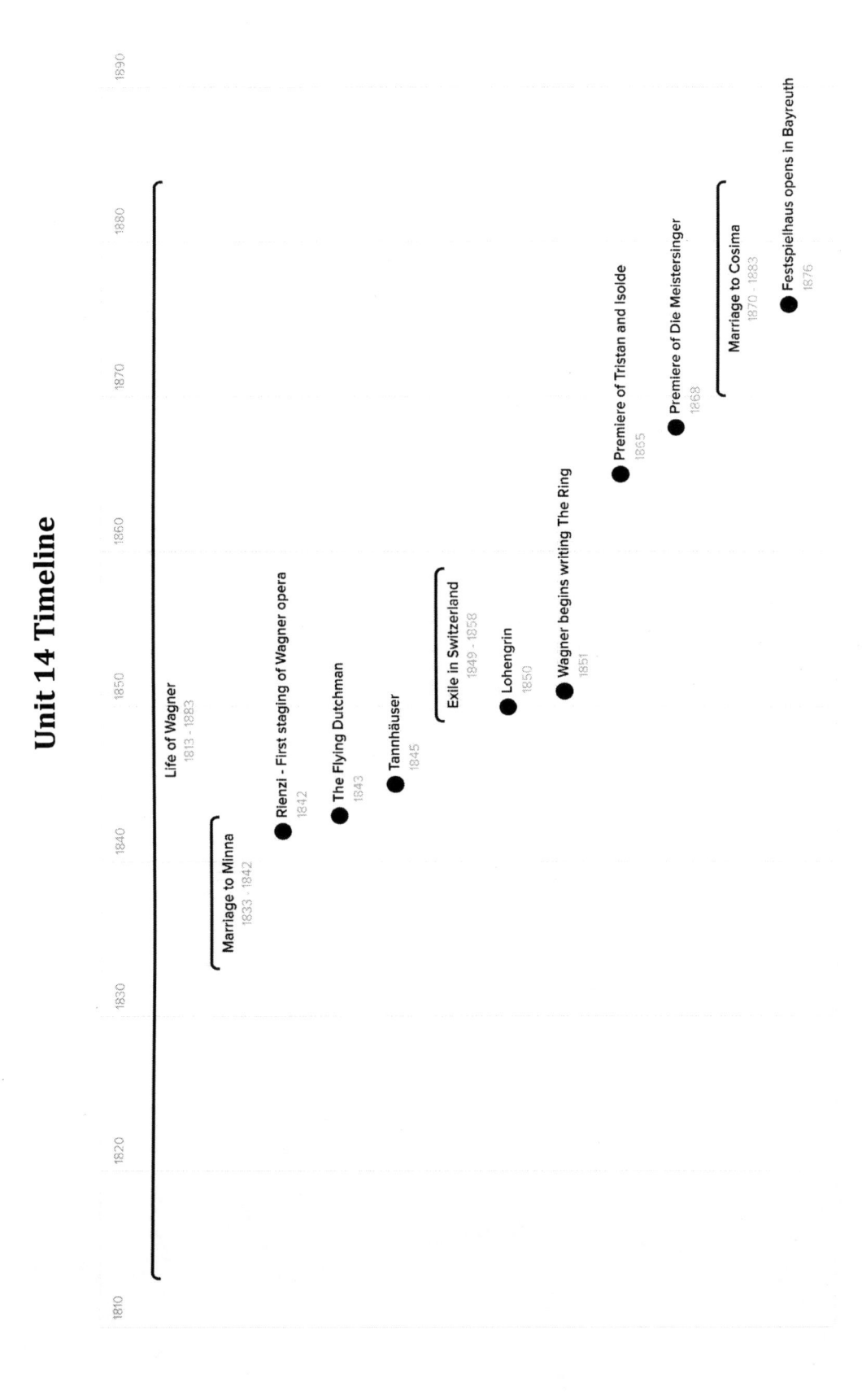

Life of Wagner
1813 - 1883

Marriage to Minna
1833 - 1842

● **Rienzi - First staging of Wagner opera**
1842

● **The Flying Dutchman**
1843

● **Tannhäuser**
1845

Exile in Switzerland
1849 - 1858

● **Lohengrin**
1850

● **Wagner begins writing The Ring**
1851

● **Premiere of Tristan and Isolde**
1865

● **Premiere of Die Meistersinger**
1868

Marriage to Cosima
1870 - 1883

● **Festspielhaus opens in Bayreuth**
1876

156 DISCOVERING MUSIC STUDENT WORKBOOK

YOUR TIMELINE

Dates →

Unit 15

Imperial Russia – A Cultural Odyssey

PEOPLE

Peter I
Peter the Great

1672-1725
Baroque

Russia
Tsar

Catherine II
Catherine the Great

1729-1796
Classical

Russia
Tsarina

Alexei I

1629-1676
Baroque

Russia
Tsar

Bortniansky
Dmitry

1721-1825
Classical

Russia
Composer

Glinka
Mikhail

1804-1857
Romantic

Russia
Composer

Balakirev
Mily

1837-1910
Romantic

Russia
Composer

Mussorgsky
Modest

1831-1889
Romantic

Russia
Composer

Borodin
Alexander

1833-1887
Romantic

Russia
Composer

Cui
César

1835-1918
Romantic

Russia
Composer

Rimsky-Korsakov
Nikolai

1844-1908
Romantic

Russia
Composer

Tchaikovsky
Pyotr Ilyich

1840-1893
Romantic

Russia
Composer

Petipa
Marius

1818-1910
Romantic

French
Ballet Master

Rachmaninov
Sergei

1873-1943
Romantic

Russia
Composer

Pushkin
Alexander

1799-1837
Romantic

Russia
Writer

Unit 15: Imperial Russia – A Cultural Odyssey

Tolstoy
Leo
1821-1910
Romantic

Russia
Writer

Dostoevsky
Fyodor
1821-1881
Romantic

Russia
Writer

Kramskoy
Ivan
1837-1887
Romantic

Russia
Artist

Surikov
Vasily
1848-1916
Romantic

Russia
Artist

Repin
Ilya
1844-1930
Romantic

Russia
Artist

Scriabin
Alexander
1872-1915
Romantic

Russia
Composer

Chekhov
Anton
1860-1904
Romantic

Russia
Playwright

Stanislavsky
Konstantin
1863-1938
Romantic

Russia
Actor, Director

Leskov
Nikolai

1831-1895
Romantic

Russia
Writer

Diaghilev
Sergei

1872-1929
Romantic

Russia
Impresario

PLACES

Constantinople (now Istanbul, Turkey)	41°00'29.66" N 28°58'42.09" E
Kyiv, Ukraine	50°27'00.36" N 30°31'24.24" E
Moscow, Russia	
Kremlin	55°45'07.28" N 37°37'03.00" E
Church of Christ the Savior	55°44'40.60" N 37°36'24.40" E
St. Petersburg, Russia	
Winter Palace	59°56'22.53" N 30°18'52.97" E
Peterhof	59°53'03.40" N 29°54'31.28" E
Catherine Palace	59°43'05.16" N 30°24'12.44" E
Kizhi	62°04'05.15" N 35°13'22.21" E

VOCABULARY

Orthodox (*ortho* = right, or correct) + (*doxos* = praise)
The name used to describe the Eastern Christian world with its spiritual center historically at Byzantium (Constantinople, today's Istanbul). The most significant Orthodox monastery is Mount Athos in Greece.

Serfdom
An ancient feudal practice that was maintained in Russian until 1861. Similar to slaves, serfs were essentially the members of society's lowest class of laborers. In Russia's vast rural economy, they were not legally free, but were bound to the land, to the Tsar (or other aristocrats), or to the Church, who essentially owned their labor and owed them only basic sustenance. Serfs had little control over their own lives, and had few rights beyond what their owners granted them.

Wanderers
Also known as the *Peredvizhniki* or the "Itinerants," this group of 19th-century Russian

artists sought to portray life in Russia as realistically as possible. Their traveling exhibitions (which earned them the name of "wanderers") helped to raise awareness of poverty and illiteracy in Russia, as well as the plight of Russia's newly freed serfs. Prominent painters included Repin, Ge, Kramskoy, and Surikov.

Mighty Handful/Fistful

Also known as the *Moguchaia kuchka* or the "Mighty Five," this group of composers is considered responsible for developing a Russian school of composition. The main members of this group, which met in St. Petersburg, were Balakirev, Rimsky-Korsakov, Mussorgsky, Cui, and Borodin.

Ballets Russes

French for "Russian Ballet," this was the troupe of Russian dancers and artists assembled by Sergei Diaghilev for a long series of performance tours to Paris. By taking advantage of the French mania for dance and for anything Russian (and therefore "exotic"), Diaghilev was able to help many Russian artists, dancers, and composers gain international fame in Europe's most important cultural capitals. The productions were innovative, elaborate, expensive, and even scandalous. Talented artists from across Europe joined in the productions as well.

DATES

988	Prince Vladimir in Kiev (Ukraine) baptizes the *Rus* as Christians.
1453	Orthodox Byzantium overtaken by Turks; Moscow becomes "Third Rome."
1825	Decembrist Uprising
1830	Pushkin's *Eugene Onegin* published.
1836	Glinka's *A Life for the Tsar* has its premiere.
1861	Tsar Alexander II abolishes serfdom.
1862	St. Petersburg Conservatory founded.
1875	Tchaikovsky's Piano Concerto performed in Boston.
1892	Premiere of Tchaikovsky's Nutcracker
1910	Diaghilev's *Ballets Russes* stages *The Firebird* in Paris.
1911	Diaghilev's *Ballets Russes* stages *Petrushka* in Paris.
1913	Diaghilev's *Ballets Russes* stages *Rite of Spring* in Paris.
1917	February and October (Bolshevik) Revolutions

162 DISCOVERING MUSIC STUDENT WORKBOOK

LISTENING

See Listening Guide at http://www.professorcarol.com/dm-listening

PUTTING IT ALL TOGETHER

1. Select and view a video performance of one of Tchaikovsky's popular ballets (or attend a live performance if you can!):

   Swan Lake

   Sleeping Beauty

   The Nutcracker

   While you are watching, think about the following questions. You might want to take some notes to help you with these questions as you watch.

   • What is your first impression of the visual aspects of the ballet (set, scenery, costumes)?

   • Does the music sound familiar to you? If so, why?

   • What aspects of the music bring the dancers on and off stage, or help make a transition from one scene to the next?

   • How many dancers appear in scene after scene? How long do the same group of dancers stay on stage?

   • Try to discover the names of some of the more astonishingly athletic moves the dancers make. Also notice which kinds of steps the ballerinas do, as opposed to the male dancers?

   • If you are watching a live performance, does applause ever break out for specific dancers during some of these amazing moments?

   • Consider the role of the *corps de ballet* (the chorus of dancers). What do they primarily do? How often are they *en pointe* (on their toes)? How strong is their ensemble (the degree to which they are exactly together in their movements)?

   • Are there vignettes of dancing (places where the characters are dancing at a ball, or waltzing, or creating some kind of dance) within the storyline?

   • How does Tchaikovsky's music set the mood in darker, spookier scenes? With a particular instrument, a silence, a change in tempo?

   • How does the staging affect these same scenes? What about costumes and props? (Hint: You may want to watch some scenes with the volume muted so that you can focus on what is happening visually.)

If possible, watch another production of this ballet, and consider the differences and similarities that you find.

2. Explore the Orthodox churches in your area. How long have they been established? Note especially if they are focused on a national community (Greek, Russian, Antiochian, Ethiopian, or other national grouping). What reasons led that group to come and build a church in that region? For example, you might find that a large number of Orthodox immigrated in the late 19th or early 20th centuries because of specific factories or industries in your area. Consider visiting the church, either outside of, or during, a service. Compile a list of questions that you might ask either a parishioner or member of the clergy, if the opportunity presents itself. Then write up your observations and new understanding of this parish and its relationship to the community.

3. Gain and understanding of one of the following Russian 19th-century authors:

> Pushkin
>
> Turgenev
>
> Gogol
>
> Chekhov

Read one work by your chosen author. It can be a short story, or something longer. In the case of Chekhov, watch a play (they are available online, or perhaps on stage near where you live). If you choose a play, try to have a copy of the play (playscript) with you as you watch. Write, in whatever form you choose, a summary of what you have experienced through this process. Try to avoid simply recounting the author's biography or the plot of what you chose.

4. Watch the film *Ivan the Terrible* (Ivan Grozny). This black-and-white film, made in 1944 and directed by famed director Sergei Eisenstein, offers a fascinating (and serious!) glimpse of the brilliant Soviet film director's approach to historical subjects. The film was made at the height of World War II and is laced with political meaning. Also, Eisenstein used film techniques far in advance of his time. What was Eisenstein's fate? (By the way, the film features a score by the great Soviet composer Sergei Prokofiev, who also wrote *Peter and the Wolf*.)

5. Study the biographies of Tolstoy and Dostoevsky. What themes and topics were their favorites? How did their personal backgrounds differ from the individuals about whom they wrote? What major political events happened in their lifetimes? How did the freeing of the serfs in 1861 affect each author? Did they write only "thick" (long!) novels, or did they also write short stories? Plays? What kind of religious beliefs did they hold?

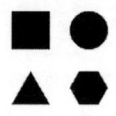

6. Study the paintings of "The Wanderers" (Itinerants). Carefully study some of their works depicting peasants. What kind of surroundings do you notice? What contrast do you see between the portraits of a single peasant and the ways in which peasants are depicted at work? Were these paintings completed before or after the liberation of the serfs in 1861? Look for information on the Tretyakov Gallery (in Moscow), one of Russia's most famous museums and permanent home to many of these works. Who was Tretyakov?

7. Research the life and music of Sergei Rachmaninov. Try to understand his place in America's musical life when he fled Russia after the 1917 Bolshevik Revolution. How did he seem to regard his new homeland? What happened to his career as a composer (in contrast to his career as a virtuoso pianist)? How has history judged his time in America? And what, generally, do people love so much about him and his music?

Unit 15: Imperial Russia – A Cultural Odyssey

VIEWING GUIDE

1. The principal key to understanding Russian music, indeed Russian culture, is to learn about _____.

2. The very name Orthodox says a great deal, since the two roots are _____, meaning _____, and _____, meaning _____.

3. The choral music in Russian Christian churches was (and still is) sung _____, which means "heads only" or unaccompanied. The melody lines were very (circle one) fluid / rigid.

4. When Western-style music (and other ideas) entered Russian Orthodoxy in the 17th century, a group called the _____ rejected the new ideas and theology and split off.

5. Russian church music was characterized by low male voices and the rich sound of _____.

6. The religious images in Orthodox churches are called _____. It is important to understand that they are venerated, not _____. To venerate means _____
_____.

7. Peter the Great was "great" in many ways, including his height, which was about _____ feet. He and his father started the trend of bringing in _____ musicians and specialists in all fields. Subsequent tsars, like _____, continued to do this.

8. Bortniansky is considered the first really prominent Russian composer, but he was, in fact _____ (nationality). This region was the _____ of Russian Orthodoxy in 988.

9. Glinka is known as the _____. His opera *A Life for the Tsar* was so successful because _____
_____
_____.

10. The Russians kept the feudal system of _____ far longer than Europeans. It was abolished in _____ (year), but many problems still lingered.

11. The Russian playwright _____ was very modern in his

ability to probe the meaning of the small actions in our daily lives. His plays include _____. The theater director _____ created an entire method of _____ that explored the psychology of the characters.

12. In the mid 19th century, a group of painters known under several names, including _____, shocked people with their realistic paintings showing the poverty of the _____ and the arrogance of the _____. The most famous of these painters was named _____.

13. Russia's most beloved author is named _____. His life bore striking resemblance to events in his greatest work, a novel in _____ called _____. While it's named after the principal male character, the real hero of the story is _____. The author himself died (how) _____.

14. Although people try to distinguish the composer _____ from a group of composers known as _____, they shared many of the same goals. But while _____ was committed to composing symphonies and concerti, the members of the other group were more focused on composing _____
_____.

15. The painter Viktor Hartmann, whose works are honored in the colorful piano cycle known as _____, died young. A short opening section called _____ is repeated throughout the piece and links the musical portraits. A very scary Russian witch is portrayed, too, and she is known as _____. She lives in a hut that stands up on _____.

16. The most famous Tsar in Russian opera has to be _____ _____. He ruled during an *interregnum* or break between the _____ dynasty and the _____ dynasty. This man seems to have been troubled by a _____. Mussorgsky's operatic version of the historical events has an extravagant _____ scene in the prologue.

17. In this opera, Mussorgsky seems to have found an important key to singing _____ in a natural and convincing way. There's also a wonderful _____ scene when the Tsar Boris sees the ghost of the murdered prince.

Unit 15: Imperial Russia – A Cultural Odyssey **167**

18. Biographers always note that Rimsky-Korsakov initially trained to become a _____. He was perhaps Russian music's best __ _____. He became a professor at the _____ _____ and despite his brilliance was always worried that he _____. Almost everyone has heard his piece called _____.

19. Late in life, Rimsky-Korsakov took on an important student, one of his _____'s friends. This young man named _____ _____ turned out to be one of the greatest Russian composers.

20. Perhaps the most famous composer to flee Russia after the Bolshevik Revolution was _____. He came to _____ where he became _____.

21. Then there was the eccentric late 19th- and early 20th-century Moscow composer named _____ who used unusual harmonies and was fascinated by _____. He explored this area by creating _____ _____. It could be considered "good" that he died before the _____ _____, because the cultural politics of its Bolshevik leader _____ would not have allowed the expression of such radical musical ideas.

22. Sergei Diaghilev's theatrical troupe called _____ was a brilliant idea. He took primarily _____ (art form) to the people who would most appreciate it, namely _____.

23. The Russian composer _____ had many hits with the *Ballets Russes*, including a ballet in 1910 about a magical creature called the _____ and another ballet in 1911 about a sad _____ named _____. This role was danced by an amazing young Russian dancer named _____.

24. There were actually two Russian _____ in 1917. The first in _____ (month) was somewhat orderly. The second in _____ (month) is usually called the _____ _____ and was led by _____ and had a drastic effect on Russian culture, including _____.

Unit 15 Timeline

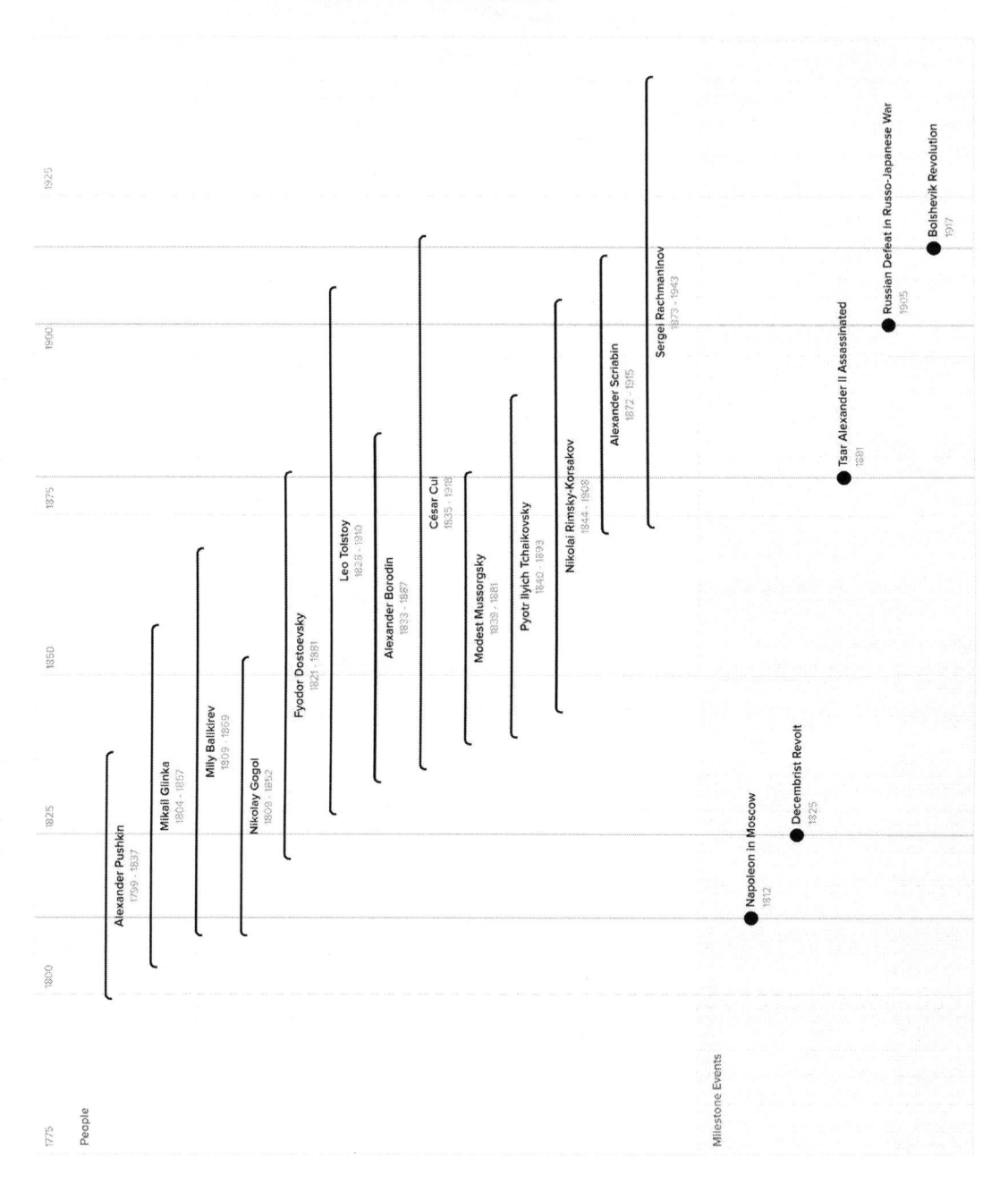

People

- Alexander Pushkin (1799–1837)
- Mikail Glinka (1804–1857)
- Mily Balikirev (1809–1869)
- Nikolay Gogol (1809–1852)
- Fyodor Dostoevsky (1821–1881)
- Leo Tolstoy (1828–1910)
- Alexander Borodin (1833–1887)
- César Cui (1835–1918)
- Modest Mussorgsky (1839–1881)
- Pyotr Ilyich Tchaikovsky (1840–1893)
- Nikolai Rimsky-Korsakov (1844–1908)
- Alexander Scriabin (1872–1915)
- Sergei Rachmaninov (1873–1943)

Milestone Events

- Napoleon in Moscow — 1812
- Decembrist Revolt — 1825
- Tsar Alexander II Assassinated — 1881
- Russian Defeat in Russo-Japanese War — 1905
- Bolshevik Revolution — 1917

Unit 15: Imperial Russia – A Cultural Odyssey

YOUR TIMELINE

Dates ⟶

Unit 16

Load Up the Wagons: The Story of American Music

PEOPLE

Billings
William
1746-1800
Classical

United States
Composer

Mason
Lowell
1792-1872
Classical

United States
Composer

Law
Andrew
1749-1821
Classical

United States
Composer

Foster
Stephen
1826-1864
Romantic

United States
Composer

Cole
Thomas
1801-1848
Romantic

American
Painter

Church
Frederic Edwin
1826-1900
Romantic

American
Painter

Unit 16: Load Up the Wagons: The Story of American Music

Durand
Asher Brown
1796-1886
Romantic

American Painter

Bierstadt
Albert
1830-1902
Romantic

American Painter

Sousa
John Philip
1854-1932
Romantic

United States Composer

Joplin
Scott
1867-1917
Romantic

United States Composer

Gottschalk
Louis Moreau
1829-1869
Romantic

American Composer

Ives
Charles
1874-1954
Modern

United States Composer

Ziegfeld
Florenz
1867-1932
Modern

United States Impresario

Berlin
Irving
1888-1989
Modern

United States Composer

PLACES

Boston, Massachusetts	42°21'36.30" N 71°03'31.97" W
Independence Hall, Philadelphia	39°56'55.95" N 75°09'00.08" W
The White House	38°53'51.63" N 77°02'11.51" W
Old Salem, North Carolina	36°05'21.00" N 80°14'37.22" W
Bethlehem, Pennsylvania	40°37'59.95" N 75°27'02.72" W
New Orleans, Louisiana	29°57'26.78" N 90°03'46.61" W
New York, New York	
Tin Pan Alley	40°44'44.93" N 73°23.05" W
New Amsterdam Theater	40°45'22.15" N 73°59'15.32" W
San Francisco, California	37°46'29.75" N 122°25'09.90" W
Danbury, Connecticut	41°24'33.69" N 73°36'52.40" W
Flanders Fields American Cemetery	50°52'26.00" N 3°27'13.00" E
Bowie, Texas	33°33'32.38" N 97°50'55.12" W

VOCABULARY

Regionalism
This American phenomenon describes the different styles of artistic traditions that sprouted in different regions across the continent throughout the nation's history. These styles have coexisted and continued to develop up to the present day.

Psalmody
This practice of composing and singing sacred music dates back to Renaissance Protestants, particularly in England and Scotland. As the name suggests, psalmody reflects a method of singing in which the melody is flexible and primarily follows the meter of the Psalms of the Old Testament. The first book published in America was a book of Psalmody, the *Bay Psalm Book*, published in 1640.

Hymnody
A general term describing the composition and singing of hymns.

Moravians
This group of Christians came from what today is the Czech Republic through Germany to Bethlehem, Pennsylvania, as missionaries, bringing with them European instruments and genres, as well as a love and respect for refined music and musical training.

Shape-Note Notation
This practice of writing the notes of the musical scale in different shapes made reading music more accessible to those who wanted to read music quickly and easily. Shape-

note notation spread by way of traveling singing masters who would cross the frontiers establishing "singing schools" for a few weeks at a time. Famous early songbooks with shape-note tunes included *Southern Harmony*, from 1835, and the *Sacred Harp* hymnal, from 1844. Quite a few of these tunes still appear in today's modern hymnals.

Handel and Haydn Oratorio Society
Established by a group of merchants in Boston, Massachusetts, in 1815, this choral society has survived to become one of the oldest continuously performing arts organizations in America. The Society produced the American premieres of such famous works as Handel's *Messiah* (in 1818), Haydn's *Creation* (in 1819), and J. S. Bach's Mass in B minor (in 1887).

Minstrelsy
Minstrelsy (Minstrel Shows) was a popular form of entertainment in the United States from the 1830s through the 1880s. Minstrel Shows were basically variety shows featuring songs, dancing, jokes, and vignettes by Caucasian performers in "black face" make-up. In exaggerated and grotesque form, they mimicked the speech, movement, and song of African slaves on Southern plantations. Despite the gross injustices and distortions of the Minstrel Shows, this form of entertainment laid a foundation for American theater and entertainment that still influences us today.

Vaudeville
An American form of stage entertainment with roots in both Minstrelsy and European opera. Vaudeville swept America from the 1880s until the rise of "talking" movies in the late 1920s. Even then, the influence of the Vaudeville show continued on radio, on the big screen (film), and eventually on television.

DATES

1730-1755	First "Great Awakening," a series of American religious revivals
1770	*The New England Psalm Singer* published.
1790-1840	Second "Great Awakening"
1815	Handel and Haydn Oratorio Society established, Boston, Massachusetts.
1843	The Christy Minstrels established in New York City.
1852	*Uncle Tom's Cabin* published by Harriet Beecher Stowe.
1859	Opera House built in New Orleans, Louisiana.
1866	Peabody Institute founded in Baltimore, Maryland.
1883	Metropolitan Opera House built in New York City.
1888	Birth of Irving Berlin

LISTENING

See Listening Guide at http://www.professorcarol.com/dm-listening

PUTTING IT ALL TOGETHER

1. Research the life of Stephen Foster. Be able to answer the following questions:

   • What kind of musical education or training did he receive?

   • Did he come from a family of musicians?

   • Was he able to earn a living from writing his songs?

   • What kinds of music did he compose?

   • What effect did the Civil War have on his music? Did he compose any well-known Civil War songs?

   • Did Foster write the texts (lyrics, words), or just the music to his songs?

   • How are his songs regarded now?

2. Research the life and works of Scott Joplin:

   Can we say for sure where and when Joplin was born?

   What "kind" of music did he make famous?

   What has been the influence of his music? How is he regarded today?

   Where is the Scott Joplin Ragtime Festival held? How often?

   Can you discover recent performances of *Treemonisha*? If so, where are these being produced? Can you find any reviews of these performances?

   Who are the "Friends of Scott Joplin"? What do they do?

3. Research the history of local arts organizations in your town or neighborhood. These may include dance troupes, choral or chamber music societies, community bands, or large symphony orchestras. Who founded them? Back in the 1880s, the founders of these organizations would likely have been a group of "society ladies"; today, it might be a group of like-minded folks in your area who want their communities to have more offerings in the arts. Such groups sometimes are also founded by local professional musicians. But frequently these organizations began with the bold visions of individual community members. Here are some places to begin:

   • the nearest orchestras, civic choruses, or opera companies

- art museums
- botanical gardens or zoos (these places often host outdoor performances)
- historical homes or villages
- libraries
- history museums
- retirement homes
- community centers
- churches or synagogues

When were these organizations founded? By whom? How was the money raised? How do they support themselves today? Who runs the organization(s) today? If you find an organization in which you are particularly interested, you may want to contact them to serve as a volunteer at a performance—hands are always needed for giving directions, handing out programs, answering questions, selling tickets, answering phones, or helping with refreshments!

4.   Discover the cultural history of your hometown or region by trying to uncover the theaters or performing arts groups that served your community in the past. Working with your local librarian, historical society, or civic museum, you should be able to find out whether there were theaters in your town, vaudeville troupes, or other musical groups regularly performing? Did the circus come regularly through your area? Does it still come through today? What about orchestras, choruses, chamber music societies, opera and theater companies? Remember: developing some sort of "cultural" life or organization was often a crucial part of "settling" the West. Even small towns without wealthy "society folks" put a high priority on bringing in cultural events because it helped put them on the map and make them a "real" town. You might be very surprised at what you uncover!

5.   What was the history behind the name of New York's "New Amsterdam" Theater? How did it get this name? How is it related to the city's history? What unique feature did the New Amsterdam Theater have on its rooftop? What was this theater's fate as the twentieth century progressed? What role did the musical *The Lion King* play in this theater's history? What is being produced there right now? How much would tickets for this production cost?

176 DISCOVERING MUSIC STUDENT WORKBOOK

VIEWING GUIDE

1. Before anyone landed in America with a violin or a conductor's baton, there was _____ ____. While much of it has been lost because it was preserved mostly by _____ tradition, we still know that it fell into _____ such as songs for working, war songs, lullabies, dances, and songs for ceremonies.

2. Understanding _____ means figuring out who settled where and brought which musical traditions with them.

3. _____ were preserved up in the _____ Mountains in states like Virginia, West Virginia, and Tennessee. They have roots that go back to England, Ireland, and Scotland and were popularly used for dancing.

4. San Gregorio de Abo is a mission located in what is today New Mexico. It was founded in _____ (date). Such missions were built to spread _____ and to teach _____ _____. The church music would have been sung in _____ (language).

5. The form of sacred singing known as _____ was important in Colonial America. The tunes were carefully taught, and offered interchangeable melodies to fit the words of the _____ from the Old Testament.

6. The _____ were Czech missionaries sent to America. They started in Pennsylvania but many of them ended up in _____ _____. These people valued European musical traditions. In Old Salem you can see an example of the kind of _____ built by a Colonial American instrument-builder named David Tannenberg.

7. The 19th-century style of singing known as _____ is done enthusiastically today by people who want to revive this musical tradition. But in the 19th century, it was the way _____ _____ _____.

8. Lowell Mason's most famous hymn tune (an arrangement) is an energetic Christmas Carol called _____. Another famous hymn written by him is _____.

Unit 16: Load Up the Wagons: The Story of American Music   177

9. Sousa is known as the _____ King all over the world. People think of him in terms of his military band career, but he actually learned some of his showmanship from conducting _____.

10. Many of America's artistic institutions, such as orchestras, opera companies, and art museums, were actually founded by groups of _____ who organized everything, and then got their _____ to write the checks. These families became patrons of the arts, replacing the patronage of European _____, which we didn't have in America.

11. An important institution in America, the _____ traveled from town to town, bringing wonders from animal acts to opera singers.

12. To get serious training, most aspiring American musicians had to travel to _____.

13. The composer Charles Ives learned creativity from his father, _____, who was the town _____. Ives is regarded today as the most significant American composer of his time, and yet, many of his friends and colleagues didn't _____ _____.

14. Charles Ives had an eclectic style, combining all kinds of melodies into his music, including _____ _____. He sent his friends copies of his _____ (which he paid out of his own pocket to publish), but he didn't get a very positive response. Today, these pieces are American treasures.

15. The poem *In Flanders Fields* was written by a _____ _____ named John McCrae. You can see the influence of this poem every time you see someone wearing a _____ to honor __ _____.

16. The festivities we call _____ in New Orleans are a direct result of American Regionalism because _____ _____. New Orleans can also call itself America's _____ of Opera.

17. On the West Coast, the musical and cultural influence of the _____ (nationality) is of great importance. These folks were brought here to work on the _____.

18. The first minstrel show was held in _____ (date). Minstrelsy was popular especially in the _____ parts of the United States. The actors wore what is called _____ made with burnt cork. We got many traditions of American entertainment from Minstrelsy, including _____.

19. The greatest songwriter of the Minstrel Era was _____ _____. He's famous for songs like (choose one) _____ _____. These tunes work well with an instrument called the _____.

20. After the Civil War, the popularity of Minstrelsy (circle one) increased / decreased. Many of the features of Minstrel shows continued into the new form of entertainment called _____.

21. One of the greatest (and longest-lived) American song writers of Vaudeville and Tin Pan Alley was _____. His family came from _____ to America. He (circle one) was / was not a highly trained musician. His first smash hit in 1911 was called _____.

22. One of his songs was also used as a theme song for a huge variety extravaganza called the _____ Follies. This show found a home in the _____ Theater in New York. That theater was renovated in recent years by the _____ and had a gala opening with the musical _____ _____.

Unit 16 Timeline

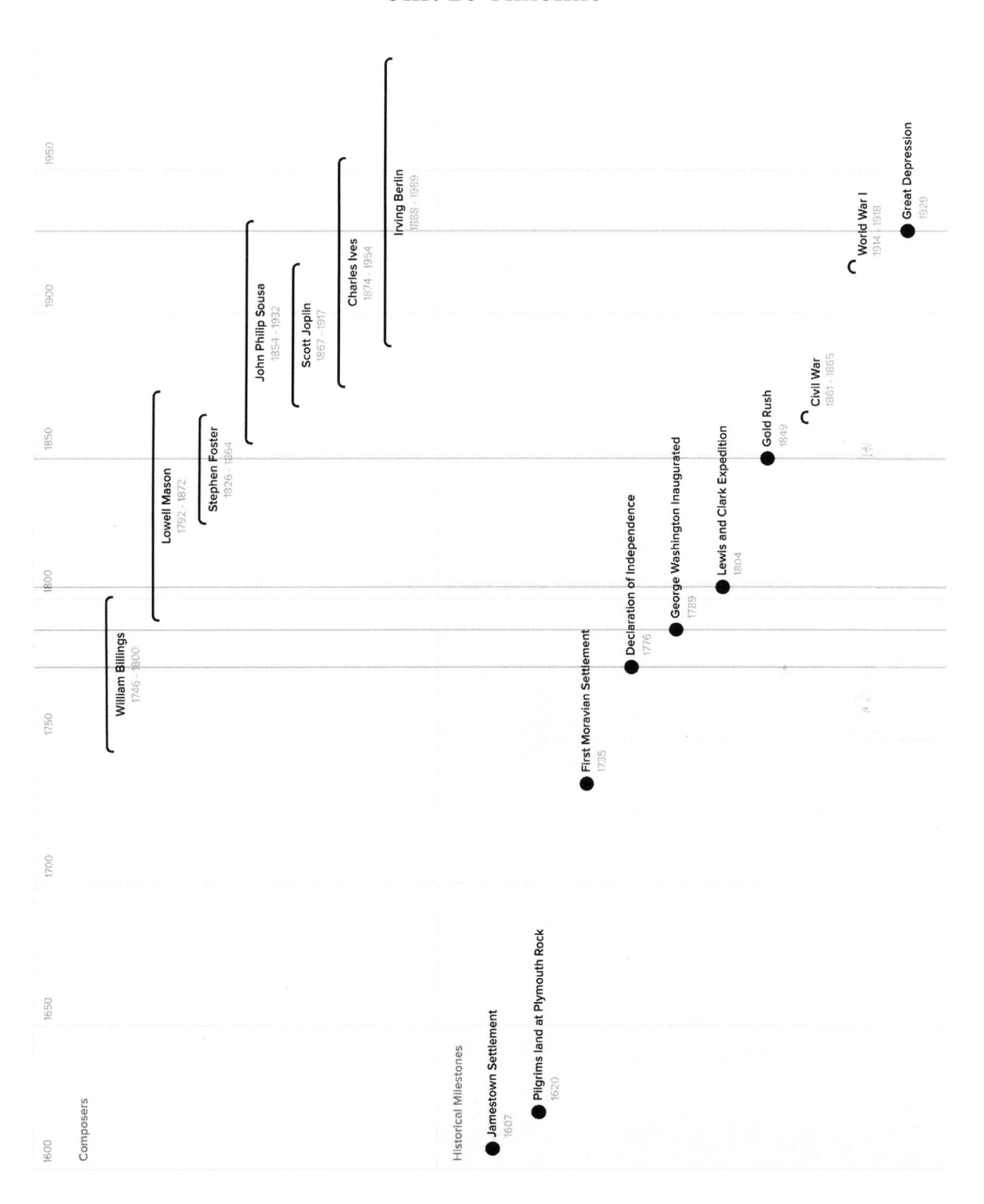

Composers:
- William Billings (1746-1800)
- Lowell Mason (1792-1872)
- Stephen Foster (1826-1864)
- John Philip Sousa (1854-1932)
- Scott Joplin (1867-1917)
- Charles Ives (1874-1954)
- Irving Berlin (1888-1989)

Historical Milestones:
- Jamestown Settlement — 1607
- Pilgrims land at Plymouth Rock — 1620
- First Moravian Settlement — 1735
- Declaration of Independence — 1776
- George Washington Inaugurated — 1789
- Lewis and Clark Expedition — 1804
- Gold Rush — 1849
- Civil War — 1861-1865
- World War I — 1914-1918
- Great Depression — 1929

180 DISCOVERING MUSIC STUDENT WORKBOOK

YOUR TIMELINE

Dates ⟶

Unit 17

Turning the Page on Western Tradition with the Explosion of War

PEOPLE

Brahms
Johannes
1833-1897
Romantic

Austria
Composer

Strauss
Richard
1864-1949
Romantic

Germany
Composer

Mahler
Gustav
1860-1911
Romantic

Austria
Composer

Mahler
Alma
1879-1964
Romantic

Austria
Composer

Debussy
Claude-Achille
1862-1918
Impressionist

France
Composer

Ravel
Maurice
1875-1937
Impressionist

France
Composer

Puccini
Giacomo

1858-1924
Romantic

Italy
Composer

Stravinsky
Igor

1882-1971
Modern

Russia, United States
Composer

Schoenberg
Arnold

1874-1951
Romantic/Modern

Austria, United States
Composer

Degas
Edgar

1834-1917
Impressionist

France
Artist

Monet
Claude

1840-1926
Impressionist

France
Artist

Cézanne
Paul

1839-1906
Post-Impressionist

France
Artist

Renoir
Pierre-Auguste

1841-1919
Impressionist

France
Artist

Manet
Édouard

1832-1883
Impressionist

France
Artist

Unit 17: Turning the Page on Western Tradition with the Explosion of War 183

Baudelaire
Charles
1821-1867
Modern/Decadent

France
Writer

Mallarmé
Stephane
1842-1898
Symbolist

France
Writer

Freud
Sigmund
1856-1939

Austria
Physician

Munch
Edvard
1863-1944
Expressionist

Norway
Artist

Bartók
Béla
1881-1945
Modern

Hungary
Composer

Kodály
Zoltán
1882-1967
Modern

Hungary
Composer

Wilde
Oscar
1854-1900
Victorian

England
Writer

Franz Joseph I
1830-1916
Romantic

Austria
Emperor

Klimt
Gustav

1862-1918
Symbolist

Austria
Artist

Diaghilev
Sergei

1872-1929
Romantic

Russia
Impresario

PLACES

Vienna, Austria	48°12'29.43" N 16°22'25.75" E
Paris, France	48°51'23.81" N 2°21'08.00" E
London, England	51°30'26.46" N 0°07'39.93" W

VOCABULARY

Fin de siècle (*Fin* = end) + (*de* = of) + (*siècle* = century)
A French term referring to the end of any century, but particularly to the years just before and after 1900. Like the phrase "turn of the century," *fin de siècle* includes the historical and cultural events that contributed to each unique historical setting—rather than just a set of dates.

Idiomatic
Any properties characteristic of the particular nature of something. For example: dialogue written in "bubbles" above a character's head could be considered "idiomatic" of a comic strip. Instrumental music that has been composed specifically to fit the way a player's hands best function on a particular instrument is said to be "idiomatic."

Impressionism
A movement in art and music characteristic of *fin-de-siècle* France. Using delicate shadings and intricate blends of shape and color, visual artists sought to capture their "impression" of an image, rather than a concrete representation. The term was coined after an exhibit in 1874, in reference to Monet's painting *Impression: Sunrise* (1872). In music, it is often associated with the works of Debussy.

Symbolism
This aesthetic style encompasses a broad range of artistic "-isms" in many different countries in the late 19th and part of the 20th century. As the term suggests, *Symbolism* simply involves using a symbol (for instance, a cross) to represent a person or idea, rather than discussing the person or idea directly.

Chinoiserie
The *fin-de-siècle* fascination with things Chinese and, by extension, anything Asian or "exotic."

Expressionism
Arising after Impressionism, this artistic movement particularly flourished in Austria and Germany at the turn of the 20th century. Expressionist artists sought to uncover the psychological "expressions" behind their images. The result is often darker and more severe than works by their Impressionist counterparts.

Sprechstimme (*sprechen* = to speak) + (*Stimme* = voice)
A vocal technique used extensively by Arnold Schönberg in works such as *Pierrot lunaire* to combine the expressive qualities of singing and speech. In *Sprechstimme*, the performer strikes the note by singing it, and then lets the note decay (as one does when speaking) rather than sustaining the pitch. The result is intended to be surprising, perhaps eerie, and expressive in a startling way. Upon first hearing, *Sprechstimme* can be confusing or off-putting to a listener.

Jugendstil (*Jugend* = youth) + (*Stil* = style)
More commonly known as *Art nouveau*, this "youthful" style of art and architecture was an early 20th-century reaction to the heavy Victorian styles popular in the late 19th century. The lines in *art nouveau* are highly curved and imitate nature. This style was most commonly seen in early 20th-century architecture as well as wrought iron decoration, furniture, jewelry, and stained glass. The famous American firm Tiffany & Co. created many pieces of jewelry and objects for domestic decoration in this style.

Ringstrasse (Ring Street)
Commonly called "The Ring," this wide boulevard runs through the heart of Vienna, Austria. The street traces the city's old garrison walls, which were destroyed in order to build the boulevard. Opened in 1860, the buildings placed on The Ring are large in scale and most have massive façades. Today The Ring is flanked on either side by museums, opera houses and theaters, public gardens, and luxury hotels and restaurants that reflect Vienna's opulent history as the cultural center of the Hapsburg Empire.

DATES

1851	First World's Fair held in London.
1853-1856	Russian-Crimean War
1860	"The Ring" (Ringstrasse) opens in Vienna.
1870-1871	Franco-Prussian War

1876	First Performance of Wagner's operatic tetralogy *The Ring* in the *Festspielhaus*
1885	Statue of Liberty arrives in New York City.
1889	Eiffel Tower is built for the *Exposition Universelle* (World's Fair) in Paris.
	North and South Dakota, Montana, and Washington admitted to the Union.
1890	Oklahoma Territory organized.
1895	Wilhelm Rontgen discovers X-Rays.
1903	Wright Brothers' first flight
1914-1918	World War I

LISTENING

See Listening Guide at http://www.professorcarol.com/dm-listening

PUTTING IT ALL TOGETHER

1. Look for a Mahler Society either in your local area or some official Mahler Society or website. When was the Society founded, and who founded it? What is the purpose of the society and what kind of information do they provide? What is required to join? Do they offer awards or fund certain projects? Assuming the society has a website, what information can you learn there that is useful to your goals in this course? Can you find branches of this society (other Gustav Mahler Societies) elsewhere in the world?

2. Research Mahler's "Composing Cabin" at Maiernegg am Wörthersee. Does it surprise you that such a spot was so important to Mahler? What is this place like today?

3. Look for an official website of the Arnold Schoenberg Center. What kind of things can you see and do at the center? Look for photographs from Schoenberg's life and read about his philosophy and goals as a teacher. Did he have other talents aside from composition? By the way, both renderings of his name are correct: Schönberg and Schoenberg. In Europe, he used the spelling Schönberg, but once he immigrated to America, he found the "oe" spelling easier to deal with.

Unit 17: Turning the Page on Western Tradition with the Explosion of War

4. Select several works of the Impressionist artists to study, starting with Monet, Manet, Degas, Cézanne, and Renoir. Have you already seen some of their paintings? From reading their biographical information, can you get a sense of which older artists influenced the younger ones? Did any of the artists have relationships with composers from our unit? When you have become familiar with the images from these artists, compare them to a few of the Expressionist works of Munch and the Jugendstil works of Klimt: what general differences do you notice?

5. Research the purpose and history behind the Paris Exposition of 1889. Learn about the fair's history from 1884-1916. What made the Eiffel Tower such a modern structure? What was unusual about it? How was it first received? How important is it today in terms of French tourism?

6. *Rite of Spring*. To get a sense of the rhythmic complexity, try counting out this pattern. For example, the first row would be counted:

1, 2, 3, **1**, 2, **1**, 2, 3, **1**, 2, 3, **1**, 2, 3, 4, **1**, 2, **1**, 2, 3

Give it a quick and steady pace with no pauses while emphasizing (or clapping on) the "1" in each group:

3	2	3	3	4	2	3
3	4	3	3	5	4	3
4	5	2	3	4	3	4
3	2	3	4	2	4	3
2	3	4	2	3	3	4

What effects do you feel after doing this (especially if done vigorously)? Imagine how you might choreograph "steps" to such a complex rhythm. Try to do some step patterns and gestures or movements to fit such rhythms.

7. What was *Art nouveau*? What appealed to people about Art Nouveau? What aspects of art did it affect? What cities were most involved in the music (hint, start with Paris and move to the capitals of Latvia, Austria, and Hungary)? Who was Alfons Mucha? At what point did the style of Art Nouveau lose its popularity, why, and to what new artistic style?

188 DISCOVERING MUSIC STUDENT WORKBOOK

VIEWING GUIDE

1. While _____ can mean the end of *any* century, it tends to mean the end of the _____ century.

2. A phrase borrowed from the title of a book on culture in Vienna at the end of the 19th century, _____, describes the conflicted atmosphere rather well.

3. Famous figures living in Vienna in the late 19th century included ____ _____.

4. The massive building project on a street now called the _____ _____ is a good symbol of the era, because _____ _____.

5. Perhaps the most famous Expressionist painting (showing a face) is entitled _____ by _____.

6. Brahms is considered a traditionalist because _____ _____ _____.

7. For some people, Brahms was the symphonist who finally stepped out of the Shadow of _____.

8. When music fits the instrument well, lies well in the player's hand, or the singer's voice, we call that kind of writing _____.

9. Brahms' heart belonged only to one woman, namely _____ _____.

10. Mahler was an intense composer. First, he was _____ (ethnicity), so to get the job as conductor at the Vienna Royal Opera, he had to _____. He married a creative young woman named _____ who, herself, was a composer. After the marriage, she (circle one) continued / quit composing. The greatest tragedy in their lives was _____.

11. Mahler's symphonies are revolutionary because _____ _____ _____ _____.

12. Debussy is called the musician who rescued France from _____

Unit 17: Turning the Page on Western Tradition with the Explosion of War

_____.

13. While he did not like the term "_____ composer," Debussy is thought of that way because _____ _____. You could almost call Debussy a musical _____ because he had much in common with poets who used _____ as symbols.

14. The painting after which the Impressionist movement was named is called _____ and was painted by _____. The word Impressionism (circle one) was / was not initially a compliment.

15. The biggest dance style sweeping across Europe at the end of the 19th century was _____.

16. Puccini was a master at presenting realistic stories on the stage. He also knew the trends, such as a fashion for things exotic (Asian) called _____. His opera _____ uses an ancient Chinese fairy tale. Other popular operas involve stories people might have recognized from the newspapers, such as the opera _____. But one of his greatest verismo (realistic) operas was a gorgeous but chilling work called *Tosca*, where the main character, an opera singer, _____ the villain and (at the end) _____.

17. People attended _____ to see exotic things and experience international cultures and modern technology.

18. _____ was a composer with two different musical lives. For decades he devoted himself to writing fantastic _____. But he also worked as a _____ and, starting around 1900, devoted himself to composing _____. His 1905 shocker _____ still rivets audiences today.

19. What is one clever way (in terms of set design) to provide water for a person singing the demanding role of Strauss' *Elektra*? _____ _____.

20. It's hard for us to realize just how amazed people were by the technology of _____ at the *fin de siècle*. People saw it mostly as a blessing that would sweep away the old inconveniences.

21. Bartok found much of his inspiration by _____

_____ with a _____ in order to capture what he heard.

22. Schoenberg began his musical career writing music that was _____ in style. His piece for string sextet called _____ is a beautiful, dream-like piece. But soon, he began to leave Common Practice Era tonality behind, writing what is called _____ music. This was a very _____ thing to do. His audience (circle one) did / did not follow him happily.

23. Then Schoenberg began writing much music using a new way of _____ called *Sprechstimme*.

24. People talk about pre- and post- _____ ears because that 1913 ballet brought in many new things. Perhaps most innovative (and disturbing to many) was the _____, created by the brilliant Russian dancer _____. He had his dancers make movements that were _____ _____.

25. The important thing to do with music that is new, and challenging, is _____ _____.

Unit 17: Turning the Page on Western Tradition with the Explosion of War

Unit 17 Timline

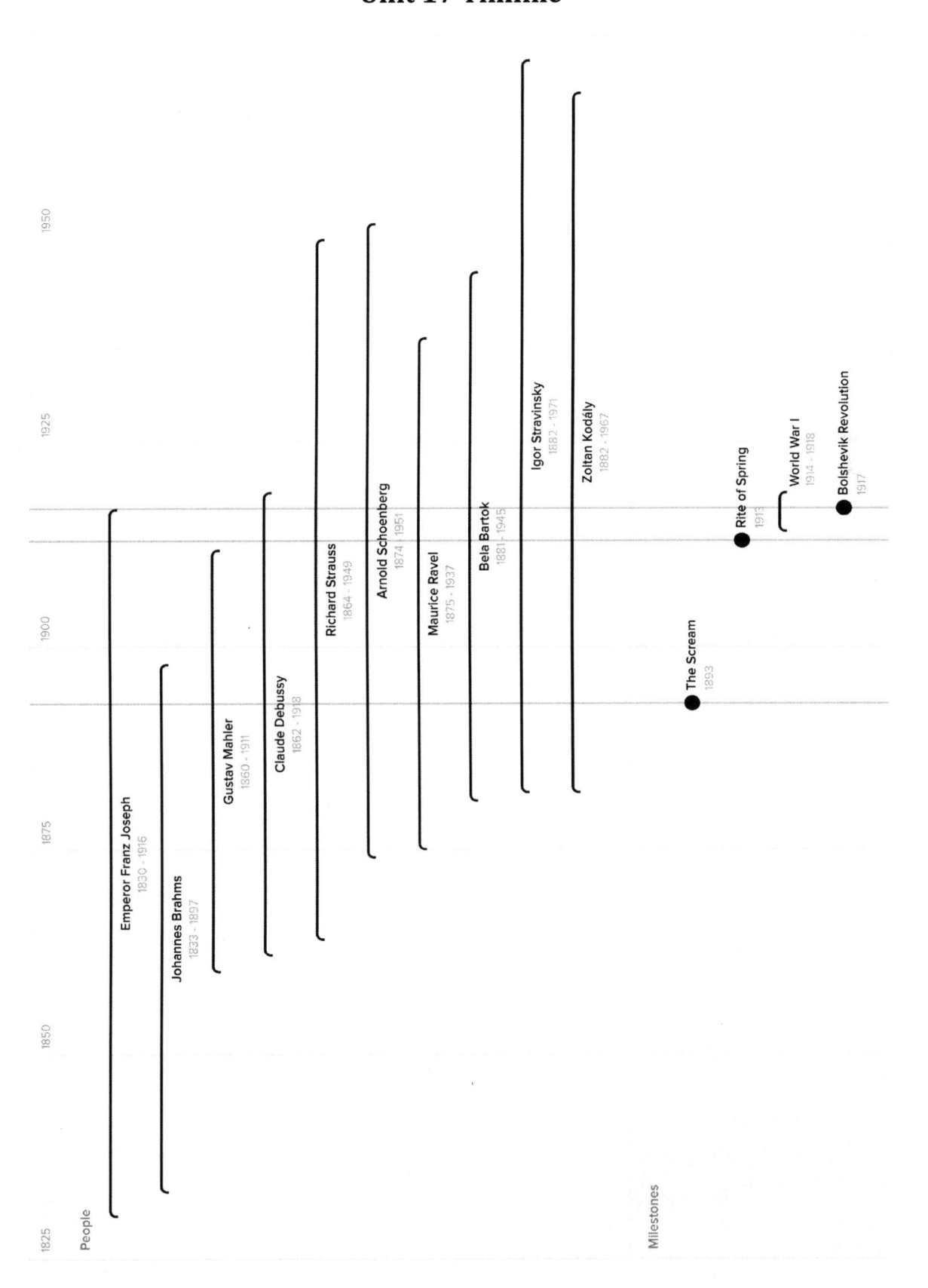

People

- Emperor Franz Joseph, 1830 - 1916
- Johannes Brahms, 1833 - 1897
- Gustav Mahler, 1860 - 1911
- Claude Debussy, 1862 - 1918
- Richard Strauss, 1864 - 1949
- Arnold Schoenberg, 1874 - 1951
- Maurice Ravel, 1875 - 1937
- Bela Bartok, 1881 - 1945
- Igor Stravinsky, 1882 - 1971
- Zoltan Kodály, 1882 - 1967

Milestones

- The Scream, 1893
- Rite of Spring, 1913
- World War I, 1914 - 1918
- Bolshevik Revolution, 1917

192 DISCOVERING MUSIC STUDENT WORKBOOK

YOUR TIMELINE

Dates ⟶

QUIZZES

UNIT 1: Using Music History to Unlock Western Culture

1. If we learn what was happening when music was written, and what the music meant to the people who heard it, then we can create a _____ for the music.

2. It's easier to absorb history if, everywhere you walk in daily life, you see _____ around you.

3. For people immigrating to the United States, the key for success has been _____ languages, whereas the key for success in Europe has been_____.

4. There's also a reverence for _____ in Europe, and people are more likely to quote _____ or make reference to them in ordinary daily life.

5. Music is a funny term because in many languages it means _____ _____ and not the _____.

6. _____ means "work" in Latin.

7. The length of a book's chapter depends on the kind of book and when it was written; similarly, the length of a _____ depends on what kind of music it is, and when it was written.

8. Songs used to be any length, but after the invention of the _____, songs rather quickly became about _____ in length.

9. Recorded music could last many minutes longer once the _____ became available. The initials mean _____.

10. Robert Schumann was not concerned about the length of his songs, but he did care about what (person) _____ thought about them! He wrote many songs in 1840 partly because _____ _____.

194 DISCOVERING MUSIC STUDENT WORKBOOK

Unit 2: Music Entwined with Great Events in Western History

1. The name of the castle where Martin Luther hid out and translated the New Testament into German: _____

2. One of the earliest technologies for recording and replaying music: _____

3. The scientific study of sound and hearing: _____

4. This type of simple tune was used in the new Protestant (Lutheran) Church services: _____

5. Inventor of the printing press: _____ When and where? _____

6. When did the events that we call "The Reformation" begin? _____ What does the word mean? _____. Who is the person credited with starting it? _____. What do we call the big division of Christianity that resulted from these events? _____ And what hyphenated term do we use loosely to identify the response of the Roman (Catholic) Church? _____

7. The level of detail possible with this kind of printing using metal plates was particularly good for mapmakers: _____

8. Printing music was more complicated than printing words because _____

9. The district in New York City filled with music publishing houses where song-writers came, hoping to get their tunes published: _____

10. What was the purpose of the Council of Trent? _____

QUIZZES 195

UNIT 3: Technology, Terminology, and Cultural Perspective

1. _____ is all around us. We just have to look at things around us (buildings, objects), analyze them, and see the patterns of repetition and contrast.

2. A piece of instrumental music written for a large ensemble with separate movements may be called a _____. A genre of music involving four players (frequently strings) is called a _____.

3. The Italian word for speed (of a piece of music in this case) is _____. The Italian word for "much" or "very" is _____, and for "less" is _____.

4. A musical term meaning generally slower or "at ease": _____ _____. A musical term for "quick": _____.

5. Extraordinary performers who seem easily to perform very difficult musical passages are known as _____.

6. The basic idea of opera goes back to _____ (time frame).

7. This word, meaning a "kind" of music, comes from the Latin word "type" or "classification": _____.

8. A _____ is a dance that was highly popular throughout Europe in the 19th century and characterized by three beats or pulses per measure.

9. A _____ is a musical genre based on the Italian word *concertare*, meaning "to agree" or "to harmonize." By the time you get to the 19th century, the relationship between the soloist and the ensemble is _____ _____.

10. The generic name (genre) given by a composer to a piece of music (circle one) does / does not completely tell you exactly what the music will be like.

UNIT 4: Fanfare and Power: The Court of Louis XIV

1. Three institutions have supported the arts in Western Culture: _____, _____, and _____.

2. Louis XIV was also known as the _____. Louis was very interested in fashion, including _____ _____.

3. What is a *faux pas*? _____. Dancing was more than a pastime. It was _____ _____.

4. Who was given the title of *Dauphin*? _____.

5. What is the name of the most beautiful formal hall in Versailles? _____. Why did Louis XIV do so much to build up Versailles? _____

6. When did Louis XIV reign? _____. How was he regarded by other monarchs who came after him? _____ _____ _____.

7. Charles Le Brun's paintings of _____ led King Louis XIV to take notice of the painter. Consequently, Le Brun became a _____ for Louis XIV.

8. The most popular keyboard instrument of the era was the _____. Why? _____

9. What was Johannes Kepler's area of study and interest? _____ _____. Another famous scientist of that time was _____.

10. Who was Molière? _____. What composer often worked with him to create wonderful productions? _____.

QUIZZES 197

UNIT 5: Sweeping Away the Renaissance into the Baroque

1. A two-part structure in opera, the first conveying information and the second expressing emotion: _____ and _____.

2. What is a *libretto*? _____. What is the root of the word? _____

3. A musical texture involving a single line: _____. A musical texture involving several voices (or melodies) woven together: _____.

4. Which dates encompass the period we're calling the Common Practice Era? _____ to _____.

5. How many players are necessary to play *basso continuo*? _____. What kinds of instruments should be used? _____.

6. A word meaning "re-birth" that describes an historical era: _____.

7. What do we call a composition that presents a melody, and then repeatedly imitates it, with contrasting episodes between these passages of imitation? _____

8. Opera literally translates as _____. The first generally recognized opera (still produced today) is called _____. Musicians love this Greek mythological story because _____ _____ _____.

9. Even tragic operas in the Baroque period were expected to end with a (in Italian) _____, which means _____ ending.

10. Which composer was among the very first to compose the new genre of opera? _____. What was he doing before he turned his talents to composing these operas? _____ _____.

UNIT 6: Liturgical Calendar, Street Parties, and the New Church Music

1. Church feasts celebrated during the year are recorded on a calendar we call the _____ calendar.

2. The four weeks prior to Christmas Eve are known as _____. In the United States today, people tend to celebrate "Christmas" during these weeks, but that's in part because our overall society is not organized around the _____.

3. What are the sources for the dramatic plots (stories) used in many oratorios? _____.

4. This genre of vocal music is based on the Italian verb "to sing": _____.

5. The long season of parties and feasting before Lent is known in Europe and South America primarily as _____ or in America as _____. How do people often dress at parties during this season? _____.

6. What are some names for the Tuesday celebrations right before Ash Wednesday? _____.

7. Oratorios that tell the story of Christ's suffering leading up to his Crucifixion are called _____.

8. Oratorios were appropriate for performance (circle one) before / during Lent? Why? _____.

9. Name two things you won't find in an oratorio that WOULD be found in an opera? _____ and _____

10. Who was one of the greatest German Baroque composers of both opera and oratorio? _____. Which oratorio do most people know by this composer? _____

UNIT 7: A Lively Journey Through the Life of Johann Sebastian Bach

1. Even though most people don't do this, it would be better to refer to Johann Sebastian Bach by his middle name, rather than his first, because _____.

2. This "Doctrine" reflects the Baroque idea of maintaining one emotion throughout a movement or section _____.

3. Sanssouci was a _____ built by _____.

4. One of Bach's older sons, _____, worked very successfully for Frederick the Great.

5. Another of Bach's sons who was quite successful, J.C. Bach, is known as the _____ (city) Bach.

6. What was Bach's musical focus while working for the Duke of Weimar? _____.

7. What is meant by the "stations of Bach"? _____ _____. At which of Sebastian Bach's stations did he remain the longest? _____.

8. What kind of young musicians did Bach supervise and teach in his post in Leipzig? _____.

9. What new, trendy establishments became a site for music-making in Bach's day? _____.

10. Name the notable German organist and composer whom Bach went hundreds of miles to see: _____. This story gets told repeatedly because Bach _____.

UNIT 8: Enlightenment, Classicism, and the Astonishing Mozart

1. This man, father of a very famous composer, was a musician too, and wrote an important treatise on the art of playing the violin: _____

2. Name one of the 18th-century thinkers known as the *Encyclopédists*: _____

3. Which 18th-century composer is known as the "Father of the Symphony"? _____.

4. An early 18th-century style that borrowed natural shapes such as pebbles, seashells, and vines: _____

5. This long German term was derived from literature and means "sensitive style": _____

6. This keyboard instrument was soft in sound, but very sensitive: _____.

7. An instrument named after the Italian terms for "loud" and "soft": _____

8. A term for light, funny 18th-century operas: _____. Behind this style of entertainment lay an old tradition of Italian street and puppet theater called _____.

9. Because this opera was a combination of funny and tragic, Mozart and his librettist _____ called (name of opera) _____ a *dramma giocoso*, which means a _____.

10. Haydn's most famous oratorio, _____, had a bilingual libretto in German and English.

QUIZZES 201

UNIT 9: Into the Abyss: The Century Struggles with Unfettered Imagination

1. The French soldier turned Emperor who attempted to conquer all of Europe, Britain, and Russia: _____

2. The Greek philosopher _____ distinguished three levels of music: _____, _____ _____ and _____.

3. A stylistic designation for an era that focuses on emotion, the individual, and the mysterious, rather than the balance and rationalism of the Enlightenment: _____

4. A literary genre that became very popular during this period: _____. Shorter versions of this genre are called _____. A sub-category of this literary genre, where the story is conveyed by an exchange of letters, is called an _____ _____.

5. What kind of literature did the Brothers Grimm collect and publish? _ _____

6. *Gemütlichkeit* could be described as _____ _____.

7. The author of *Ivanhoe*: _____. The author of Frankenstein: _____.

8. The American Romantic poet who also embraced the supernatural and spooky: _____

9. An author in Berlin who wrote short stories about fantastic events, many of them built around musicians: _____.

10. Arguably the most significant German Romantic author, _____, became famous in 1774 with an early book entitled _____, a love story with a drastic ending. But his most significant creation was a two-part play called _____ centered on a wager (a bet) between _____ _____ _____.

UNIT 10: Beethoven as Hero and Revolutionary

1. Name the Romantic artist who painted many striking, even eerie, paintings of nature, especially the moon: _____

2. Which French leader did Beethoven initially admire? _____

3. What caused Beethoven to change his mind about this leader? _____

4. What is the "Heiligenstadt Testament"? _____

5. To whom was this testament written, and for what reasons? _____

6. In music, what is a "motive"? _____

7. Name Beethoven's only opera: _____. What is one of the main themes of its plot? _____

8. The 19th-century tendency to create oversized "memorials" to great men in art, music, and culture can be called _____.

9. Beethoven's deafness did not prevent him from writing music, but it did make it difficult for him to _____

10. We can learn a lot about Beethoven's actual note-by-note creative process because he left behind many pages of _____.

UNIT 11: Salons, Poetry, and the Power of the Song

1. German for "song": _____

2. In what social setting was "song" most often performed? _____

3. What style of furniture would you find in middle-class German homes of the early 19th century? _____

4. Which German female composer whose works have recently become popular was also sister to a famous composer? _____

5. In which German city would you find the *Gewandhaus*? _____. What does the word mean? _____

6. Which of the composers in this unit became the conductor and music director there? _____

7. Name the famous German poet and thinker who wrote *Faust* but also wrote the text for many *Lieder* (and he was friends with Beethoven): _____

8. What features distinguish a ballad? _____

9. _____, perhaps Romanticism's most famous ballad, was written by Goethe. It tells a story about a _____ child and was set to music by both Loewe and Schubert.

10. _____ was a brilliant Viennese composer of song and symphony who died very young. Most of his career took place within the walls of aristocratic _____.

UNIT 12: A Tale of Four Virtuosi and the Birth of the Tone Poem

1. Name the famous violinist who invented new playing techniques for his instrument in the early 19th century: _____

2. Which famous pianist was inspired by seeing this violinist perform in 1831? _____.

3. Which famous Polish-born virtuoso composed almost all of his music for the piano only? _____

4. What kind or style of piece is a "nocturne"? _____
_____

5. Name a Polish national dance: _____

6. This kind of piece is meant as a "study": _____

7. This French artist was a friend of Chopin and Georges Sand: _____

8. Who was the "Swedish Nightingale"? _____. What was her connection to the United States? _____
_____.

9. Which French composer wrote the *Symphonie fantastique*? _____. What or who inspired him to do it? _____
_____

10. What is a "tone poem"? _____
_____

UNIT 13: Nationalism and the Explosion of Romantic Opera

1. This type of 19th-century opera involves a chorus, an historical plot, usually five acts, and lots of pageantry: _____

2. What do we call the new style of dancing for women that, at first, was "spooky" but later became standard ballet technique? _____

3. *Bel canto* literally means _____.

4. What do we call the depiction of life and tragedy in a "realistic" way on stage, particularly in late 19th-century opera? _____

5. A highly popular social dance in triple meter from the 18th century involving limited physical contact between the dancing partners: _____

6. This kind of social dance, popular throughout the whole 19th century, required holding on tightly, plus "locking eyes" to avoid dizziness: _____

7. *Singspiel* literally means _____. We in America like to call this kind of operatic format a _____.

8. This famous Italian operatic composer was hailed as a hero of *Il Risorgimento*: _____

9. The ballet *Giselle* is his classic work, but most people know Adolph Adam for a Christmas song called _____.

10. The most famous early German Romantic opera by Weber is called: _____. What happens in the scariest scene? _____

UNIT 14: The Absolutely New World of Wagner

1. Name the German king who supported Wagner's work financially. _____

2. Which German castle did Martin Luther "visit" and Wagner use as the setting for his opera Tannhäuser? _____

3. *Gesamt*= _____, *Kunst*= _____, *Werk*= _____

4. What is a *Leitmotiv*? _____
_____
_____

5. What is a *Meistersinger*? _____
_____

6. What is the *Festspielhaus*? _____. Where is it located? _____. Why was it built? _____
_____
_____

7. Describe two special features of the *Festspielhaus*: _____
_____
_____

8. Which 20th-century dictator appropriated Wagner's music for his own political use? _____
_____

9. Wagner wrote many of his essays as well as ideas for *The Ring* while in exile in _____ (country). He was there from 1849 until 1861 because _____.

10. Which German river plays an important part in Wagner's operas? _____

UNIT 15: Imperial Russia – A Cultural Odyssey

1. Which Russian composer wrote *The Nutcracker*, as well as other famous ballets? _____

2. Orthodox means _____.

3. The Tsars loved to import their culture, and they were fond of appointing *Kapellmeisters* who were _____ (nationality). Finally, though, a native-born composer named _____ _____ was appointed to this high post. He was not Russian, actually, but _____ (nationality).

4. *Moguchaia kuchka* means _____. Rather than music, what kinds of professions did the members of the *kuchka* have? _____
_____

5. The sound of _____ filled cities and villages. These important symbols of Russian Christianity and culture were destroyed after the Second _____ Revolution of _____ (year).

6. What was the *Ballets Russes*? _____
_____ Where did they perform? _____

7. Which early 19th-century Russian composer is considered the "Father of Russian Music"? _____

8. In the Christian church, what is an icon? _____
_____. To use proper terminology, an icon is not drawn or painted, but rather is _____; an icon is not viewed, or looked at, but is _____. And an icon is not worshipped, but is _____.

9. What kind of themes did painters known as "The Wanderers" ("The Itinerants") portray on canvas? _____
_____
_____

10. Which Russian city was called the "Third Rome"? _____

UNIT 16: Load Up the Wagons: The Story of American Music

1. What is "Hymnody"? _____
_____ Psalmody? _____
_____

2. Many fiddle tunes were brought into which region of America? _____
_____

3. How did Chinese music find its way to the West Coast of America? ___
_____

4. *Southern Harmony* and *Sacred Harp* were examples of what kind of notation: _____.

5. In which U.S. city was the first American opera house built? _____
_____

6. Which American composer, now famous for his symphonies and songs, worked as a pioneer in the insurance industry?
_____

7. Which composer still popular today wrote American *Lieder* throughout the Civil War period? _____

8. For what genre of music is John Philip Sousa most famous? _____
_____

9. Old Salem, North Carolina was home to this group of music-loving missionaries from Eastern Europe (who first arrived in Bethlehem, Pennsylvania): _____

10. Which American theater entrepreneur made the New Amsterdam Theater famous? _____. What musical was staged to celebrate the restoration of this theater? _____
_____

UNIT 17: Turning the Page on Western Tradition with the Explosion of War

1. What time period is known as the *fin de siècle*? _____

2. Which composer developed *Sprechstimme*? _____

3. Which composer best represents, to us, the "Impressionist" movement? _____. Would he have liked our saying this? Yes / No

4. Name two Impressionist painters: _____

5. Which artistic movement, very much in contrast to Impressionism, developed next in Austria and Germany? _____

6. In which city will you find the *Ringstrasse*? _____

7. What is *chinoiserie*? _____

8. What cataclysmic event began in 1914? _____

9. Which German composer wrote a symphony that was loosely regarded by some as "Beethoven's Tenth"? _____

10. What is the name of the World War I poem that gave us the Red Poppy as a symbol of War Dead? _____

SUGGESTED ANSWERS FOR VIEWING GUIDES

UNIT 1: USING MUSIC HISTORY TO UNLOCK WESTERN CULTURE

Please see the Listening Exercises (in lieu of a Viewing Guide).

UNIT 2: MUSIC ENTWINED WITH GREAT EVENTS IN WESTERN HISTORY

1. 1920s; the songs played on the radio determined which songs would be popular; now it's possible to hear virtually any kind of music any time one wishes.
2. Printing press in Mainz, Germany; Gutenberg; paper; parchment.
3. Chinese
4. hand-copying done by trained people, often monks (as well as woodblock)
5. animal skins; 300
6. 30,000; nine million
7. by hand / in manuscript (by copyists working in scriptoria).
8. no
9. mapmakers
10. backwards
11. lithography
12. At first it made songs more popular, so publishers sold even more sheet music. But since it was now possible to hear music without learning to play and sing it, the gramophone hurt sales of printed music.
13. New York City; music publishing
14. From the clanking piano sounds floating out of the windows of publishing houses, where songwriters presented new songs, hoping for publication.
15. acoustics
16. Pythagoras
17. Greek theater builders considered acoustics / Medieval architects placed big ceramic urns to affect acoustics, etc.
18. French; sun; Classical mythology / Apollo.
19. Copernicus; Kepler
20. The Enlightenment; the supernatural / the individual / the emotional / the psychological / the sublime

UNIT 3: TECHNOLOGY, TERMINOLOGY, AND CULTURAL PERSPECTIVE

1. shape / structure / construction / design (based on repetition and contrast)
2. buildings / architecture in general / any physical space or object
3. distinct sections within a larger piece of music
4. top left, above where the music itself begins
5. happy
6. walking tempo
7. at ease (slowly); broadly
8. fast; vivere (to live)

9. meno; molto
10. No; in earlier eras (Renaissance, Baroque), tempos or speeds were "understood" based on the kind of music being performed. It was an issue of style.
11. a champion athlete such as an Olympic gymnast or pole vaulter
12. style
13. kind or type of thing. (It comes from the Latin *genus*, meaning birth, family, or nation.)
14. these things frequently overlap. A piece may be called one thing, but function as another thing. Plus the meanings of these genres may change throughout history, or from one composer to another. A composer can call a piece anything he or she wishes, in fact!
15. large
16. No, as long as there are four players (or singers).
17. Greeks / Greek drama / Classical antiquity
18. to agree / to harmonize / to reach an accord together
19. It depends. It can be small (5 - 10 players), or medium sized (20 - 30 players), or as big as the modern orchestra (c. 100 players) or even bigger (orchestra and choirs combined). Generally speaking, ensembles have increased in size throughout Western music history, at least until the First World War, when almost everything drew back in size and scope. Today a modern orchestra will be about 85-100 players.

UNIT 4: FANFARE AND POWER: THE COURT OF LOUIS XIV

1. Church, Court, and Theater
2. We choose to hear voluntary music, either by playing it ourselves, listening to others play it, or turning on a piece of digital technology, or older technology like a radio, tape player, or phonograph. Involuntary music comes to us whether we want it or not, standing in an elevator, pumping gas, going into a hotel lobby or restaurant, or hearing it blared from a car parked next to us.
3. Women weren't allowed to sing in public
4. Versailles
5. Maître de chapelle / Kapellmeister
6. harpsichord
7. Absolutism; Louis XIV / Frederick the Great / Catherine the Great / Joseph II of Austria
8. château; hunting lodge
9. dancers, singers, musicians, painters, playwrights, choreographers, costume and set designers, stage directors, etc.
10. Sun King; Classical Mythology and Apollo
11. Charles Le Brun
12. solar system; establish an Academy of Science
13. dancer; faux pas; the dance steps stayed simple enough for the King
14. The Hall of Mirrors; the signing of the treaties that ended both the Franco-Prussian War and the First World War
15. Molière
16. rising and dressing, eating, and preparing for sleep at night

17. French Overture
18. Versailles; palace interior; gardens

UNIT 5: SWEEPING AWAY THE RENAISSANCE INTO THE BAROQUE
1. Common Practice Era; was "practiced" (played, performed, and perceived) in a certain way
2. (choose three) Music had a clear pulse / the musical scales used were primarily two: we call them major and minor / music had a clear melody line supported by a bass line / music was composed in specific, predictable forms, created by sections of contrast and repetition / music was played on the same instruments we more or less recognize today / these instruments were played in a traditional manner, appropriate to the instrument.
3. Florence; Dante / Boccaccio / Brunelleschi
4. opera
5. rebirth
6. Humanism
7. Monteverdi; highly polyphonic (complex web of melody lines); monophonic (monody, or single melody line—recitative style)
8. Fable (favola) in music.
9. play; sung
10. choosing specific instruments to get the desired sound
11. St. Mark's Cathedral in Venice
12. A beloved mythological figure whose powers to charm through music and poetry were legendary. (He was the son either of a Thracian king or the god Apollo, depending on the version. His mother was one of the Muses, Calliope.)
13. lieto fine
14. Greek mythology / Classical history
15. misshapen pearl; was not
16. single-line melody, or one musical line is sung or played; polyphonic (with two, three, then four melody lines sounding simultaneously)
17. manuscript
18. two players, one playing a chording instrument, like a lute, harpsichord, organ and the other playing an instrument like a cello or bassoon, which can play a low sustained bass line.
19. toccata; fantasia
20. highly developed piece of music where a melody is presented and imitated in several voices with contrasting episodes in between
21. information; the part where the emotions are sung
22. opera seria; intermezzos (intermezzi)
23. the aristocracy, kings, noblemen (in short, only the rich)
24. opus; opera

SUGGESTED ANSWERS FOR VIEWING GUIDES

UNIT 6: LITURGICAL MUSIC, STREET PARTIES, AND THE NEW CHURCH MUSIC
1. sacred; secular; it is associated with church performance or has a recognized part in the worship service.
2. he wanted the new Protestant songs (hymns) to be lively, metrical, inspiring, and accessible, so he often looked to popular and folk tunes.
3. a worship service (church service); Communion (also known as The Lord's Supper, Bread and Wine, or the Eucharist)
4. the Feast days, or days of celebration within the church year; Christmas or All Saints' Day; Easter, Good Friday, Maundy Thursday, Palm Sunday, Ash Wednesday
5. it was hot, and there was a danger of spreading diseases; Lent was a season of fasting and penitence (devotion).
6. indulge in rich foods and lots of entertainment beforehand; opera; because opera is a social, glamorous, and extravagant art form; masked balls
7. New Orleans; the region was settled by French Catholics, so the Liturgical Calendar shaped social life and entertainment.
8. new operas; new oratorios; oratorios had religious topics and no staging or acting, so they were appropriate for penitential (fasting) seasons.
9. church sanctuary itself (not woven into the services); within the church services
10. two; a type of sermon
11. Old Testament; they are more dramatic. They portray events like the bestowing of the Ten Commandments, the Parting of the Red Sea, plus many floods, battles, murders, assassinations, struggles of all kinds.
12. Passions

UNIT 7: A LIVELY JOURNEY THROUGH THE LIFE OF JOHANN SEBASTIAN BACH.
1. middle; Sebastian; first; Johann
2. Doctrine; Affections; stay joyful; switch to something sad, dark, slow
3. Stations; outgrew his jobs, or was too advanced or modern for them, or was not permitted to write the kinds of music he wanted to compose
4. Weimar; church organist or church musician; he sought a new job without permission to do so.
5. Cöthen (Köthen); the music-loving duke died
6. Leipzig; boys in the boys' choir; St. Thomas Church (Thomaskirche); Coffee Houses; public concert
7. organ; bellows boys; bellows; air; pipes; electricity (electric motors)
8. clavichord; was not; it was extremely soft; control the volume (dynamics) or sensitivity of each sound
9. C.P.E. Bach; Frederick the Great; Berlin; fortepiano (or pianoforte)

UNIT 8: ENLIGHTENMENT, CLASSICISM, AND THE ASTONISHING MOZART
1. high skill level, increased complexity, and musical ideas all expanding, and then, suddenly, a collapse to a much simpler style.
2. classical
3. Alberti bass
4. Monarchs (Monarchy); Prussia; Russia; Austria

5. Art (paintings, sculpture)
6. rococo
7. galant; pleasantness, naturalness, diversion, light-hearted emotion; Watteau
8. Sturm und Drang
9. sensitive; Affections
10. sons; Prussian; Frederick the Great
11. clavichord
12. the hammer, the padding on the hammer, the tuning pins, the bridge, the sounding board, the escapement mechanism (double-escapement), the cast-iron frame
13. harpsichord; fortepiano (pianoforte); upright piano
14. Thomas Jefferson
15. Prague (today's Czech Republic)
16. Italian (Italianate); France
17. clarinet
18. Turkish
19. buffa; seria; Singspiel; The Magic Flute
20. Lorenzo da Ponte; The Marriage of Figaro (Le nozze di Figaro)
21. He worked contentedly for many years for Count Esterhàzy. He enjoyed job stability and handled being a "servant" well.
22. symphonies; baryton
23. Let there be Light (very quiet chorus leading up to it, and then a huge burst of sound on the word "light"); or recitative "painting" animals in sound.

UNIT 9: INTO THE ABYSS: THE CENTURY STRUGGLES WITH UNFETTERED IMAGINATION

1. literature
2. the supernatural, the other-worldly, the spooky; histories; legends and folk or fairy tales; works of art like operas, plays, paintings, novels, poems
3. (choose) vernacular language of French, or any language related to French, and later any language stemming from Latin, a medieval verse or prose work, especially concerned with chivalry, a novel, an adventure story, or even "the sublime" or things that we cannot fully understand or explain, but know are real.
4. Charles Dickens; A Tale of Two Cities; "It was the best of times; it was the worst of times."
5. The Enlightenment; coronated; Notre Dame
6. David; 1812; burning Moscow and leaving Napoleon and his troops without supplies for the winter; Hitler / the Germans
7. Biedermeier; Spitzweg; Gemütlichkeit; Congress of Vienna
8. turned to extreme emotions / described the world around them (etc.); emotional, supernatural, fantastic, even dangerous (threatening)
9. musica mundana; spheres; musica humana; musica instrumentalis
10. E.T.A. Hoffmann; Mozart; "inexpressible longing"; The Nutcracker
11. Sir Walter Scott; Lord George Gordon Byron; Mozart
12. The Grimm Brothers (The Brothers Grimm); they are about bewitched and fantastic creatures, supernatural, the battle of Good against Evil, villains, and spooks.

SUGGESTED ANSWERS FOR VIEWING GUIDES 215

13. Frankenstein; The Raven; Edgar Allan Poe
14. madness (insanity); Lucia di Lammermoor
15. Johann von Goethe; The Sorrows (Sufferings) of Young Werther; epistolary novel; one way; suicide; Werther
16. Weimar; well; Faust; bargain (bet or wager); Devil (Mephistopheles, Mefisto); Devil; moment (day) of pure joy and contentment; Devil; soul
17. Schiller

UNIT 10: BEETHOVEN AS HERO AND REVOLUTIONARY

1. he represents a new kind of "Romantic" artist—an individual struggling against society / he was a genius whose talents were too great to be fully appreciated / he was a hero whose music (posthumously) set a new standard against which subsequent music would be compared.
2. c. 19 (actually the best answer is 18, as he was 5 months shy of 19 (he was born 16 December 1770; the French Revolution begins July 14, 1789)
3. the patronage system where a count, for example, would determine what an artist created
4. Somewhat, but nothing like Mozart's or Bach's.
5. He was not well connected, he didn't have the proper upbringing or preparation socially for the big city, his temperament rebelled against the role that was expected of him.
6. Johann von Goethe; no, they did not agree on many things, including the appropriate way to defer to aristocracy.
7. At first he was thrilled, but he was later disappointed when Napoleon began grabbing power and crowned himself Emperor.
8. A rescue opera / a Singspiel; four overtures
9. the loyalty of a wife, bravery in face of danger, political oppression, hope triumphing over desperation, the excitement of a last-minute rescue
10. more difficult for audiences / more extreme / more introverted / less automatically attractive / less likely to please
11. sitting on a "throne" like a god of some kind, with an eagle, and other monumental symbols
12. It was done years after Beethoven's death, and it shows the powerful figure Beethoven had become—no longer a man who simply wrote music, but a kind of god-like figure who towered over the world of music, knowing all, seeing all, directing all!
13. Healing City; to seek a cure for his deafness; Testament; it is both a highly emotional letter that tells us much about Beethoven's state of mind and a statement of the new "Romantic" views of nature, God, and fate.
14. manicured, sculpted, trimmed Baroque gardens; open, free, wild, overgrown "Romantic" parks (although still trimmed by gardeners to get the right look!).
15. longer, bigger, more monumental in scope, more intense harmonies, darker in tone, sometimes heroic, and always emotional, very specific indications, unexpected structures and unexpected passages, less lyrical and more dependent on patterns (motives) that aren't really melodies, formed according to his own rules.
16. In his later works, he put these terms into the vernacular (his own language of

German) rather than just Italian.
17. sketches; his musical and compositional ideas, his creative processes
18. The moon was mysterious, sublime, inexplicable, plus the moon made a mesmerizing focal point. And people were very interested in the moon, astronomically, in those days.
19. Father of Modern Astronomy; Uranus

UNIT 11: SALONS, POETRY, AND THE POWER OF THE SONG
1. lute; Queen Elizabeth of England; 1603; Shakespeare; John Dowland
2. "words carefully chosen and arranged on a page."
3. The audience must understand the words; the words should connect emotionally with the listener; the song needs to be presented in an appropriate environment.
4. small or intimate
5. read aloud as a poem; set to music as a song
6. the supernatural, lost love or disappointed love, nature, legends, adventure stories, medieval themes, folk themes
7. a parlor or room where invited guests would gather to hear the newest poetry and literature read, and to enjoy the newest pieces of music
8. It has a narrator; it has actual characters who address one another; it narrates objectively and begins *in media res*—suddenly, without a lot of explanation; it draws no moral conclusion.
9. in the middle of things or midstream
10. four; the father, the boy, the Erl-King, and the narrator (and if you count the horse, you get a fifth character)
11. early 19th century
12. he was frustrated in his attempts to marry Clara Wieck, so the bitter story would have appealed to him (plus Heine was a great poet).
13. the happiness doesn't last, and the poems become progressively sadder or angrier.
14. "I don't complain"; using low, pounding chords, setting up an insistent and angry musical accompaniment
15. the poet's resignation to the situation, and a beautiful piano postlude.

UNIT 12: A TALE OF FOUR VIRTUOSI AND THE BIRTH OF THE TONE POEM
1. the excitement of watching someone do something physically "impossible" / the glamour and star status of such people (for example, super-star athletes)
2. Paganini
3. he had an unusual appearance, especially his hands, and people were fascinated by him / he seemed to be self taught, which gave rise to the rumor that "the devil" had taught him / his technique in playing the violin was radical and new; The Romantic era promoted the idea of the "creative individual" and virtuosi fit the bill!
4. human achievement, something from "beyond" or even the supernatural / a gift a person was born with, largely unexplained. Art had a secret message for us, and only artists could understand certain things. Artists were no longer servants and craftsmen, but specially endowed visionaries who could point the way into the future.

SUGGESTED ANSWERS FOR VIEWING GUIDES

5. fifteen
6. Franz Liszt
7. was elegant, handsome, charming to the ladies.
8. concert pianist / recitalist / performer; Europe and even Russia
9. Chopin, George Sands, Delacroix
10. City of Lights; He had started the idea of public street lighting with candles and torches. This public lighting gave Paris its first nightlife and made it the envy of Europe.
11. Weimar; compose more, especially tone poems (symphonic poems); Rome; focus on religious study and preparation, ultimately becoming an Abbé / writing sacred music
12. virtuoso performers; Jenny Lind; Sweden
13. It was more poetic, more subdued, less bombastic, less concentrated on thrills and more on expression (although there were plenty of thrills).
14. to study; a piece used as an exercise in order to master difficult performing techniques
15. Polish; Paris
16. no
17. a piece of instrumental music that tries to paint a picture of something, either a place, a thing, an atmosphere, or even an emotion
18. Irish; John Field
19. works like symphonies, operas, string quartets, oratorios
20. Jewish
21. St. Paul; Elijah
22. Johann Sebastian Bach
23. painter, or watercolorist
24. Fanny Mendelssohn Hensel
25. the orchestra conductor
26. music performed by a variety of players, including singers, violinists and pianists, small ensembles, wind and brass players too! It was more like a variety show.
27. instrumental pieces that tell a story (without words) or describe (paint in music) a place, person, thing, or emotion
28. Hector Berlioz; his passion for an English Shakespearean actress named Harriet Smithson
29. a house where Liszt lived, on a hill above Weimar, where a stream of fellow musicians and well-known figures visited and also stayed.
30. his ideas were more advanced than the people around him / he conducted controversial music, both his and the new music of other composers.
31. Richard Wagner

UNIT 13: NATIONALISM AND THE EXPLOSION OF ROMANTIC OPERA
1. Louis XIV; minuet; waltz
2. to dance
3. Beethoven
4. Romantic; Classical; Classical; Romantic
5. spooky, supernatural, mysterious / characters who were supernatural

6. sentimentalism; Gothic / supernatural / Romantic; Willis
7. mad; Lucia di Lammermoor; Sir Walter Scott
8. motives / Leitmotifs
9. French; [French] Grand; weddings, processionals, coronations, feasts
10. the supernatural, the spooky, the mysterious; rescue / redemption
11. 1821; it featured lots of German folk elements, like the forest, hunting, folk dancing, and the sound of a men's chorus (*Männerchor*). It also used several traditional German superstitions in the plot.
12. Franco-Prussian War; 1870-71; 1861
13. musical (Broadway musical)
14. "Ordinary" opera has sung recitatives (that is, information or conversation will be sung in rhythmically free melody). In *Singspiel*, or dialogue opera, the information, or conversation is spoken, as in a play. [In both forms of opera, the arias (songs), duets, and choruses are sung.]
15. Absolutely not! (There are many tragic and sad endings.)
16. Rossini, Donizetti, Bellini
17. bel = beautiful + canto = singing, so "beautiful singing"
18. overtures; ensembles
19. Nebuchadnezzar; "Va pensiero" (Fly, Thoughts, on Wings of Gold)
20. A scene in an opera (started in the 19th century) that weaves arias, duets, choruses together, more or less seamlessly
21. The fight by Italian nationalists to overthrow Austrian power and unify Italy into a country.
22. Viva Vittorio Emanuele, King (Re) of (d') Italy (Italia); To make a cry in public for an Italian King (and a united Italy) was politically dangerous. Using Verdi's name as a "code" was safer.
23. Spanish.
24. with the on-stage murder of Carmen; verismo
25. The Metropolitan Opera Saturday Matinees (from New York City); Texaco

UNIT 14: THE ABSOLUTELY NEW WORLD OF WAGNER
1. Rhine river / the gold from the Rhine / the problems of the gods from Valhalla; Germanic, Nordic / Scandinavian
2. less than ideal, somewhat unstable, artistic through his stepfather
3. false
4. Hitler was enthusiastic about Wagner's music and the ideas in his essays.
5. The Flying Dutchman; he was caught in a storm while fleeing his conducting position at Riga.
6. not successful or pleasant (he couldn't find success)
7. Wartburg; 1517; translate the New Testament; competed in the famous medieval "Singers' Wars."
8. Gesamtkunstwerk
9. Franz Liszt; Bavarian King Ludwig II (Mad Ludwig, or The Dream King)
10. Leitmotiv (leading or guiding motive); characters, things, and ideas
11. underneath; the huge sound of his big orchestra would not overwhelm the singers

SUGGESTED ANSWERS FOR VIEWING GUIDES 219

on stage, but would blend together and make a perfect balance with their voices; Wagner tuba
12. false (he wanted their ears, brains, and imaginations fully engaged!)
13. 19; was not
14. *Das Rheingold*; his operas needed to be seen, heard, and experienced completely, and short excerpts on a CD or YouTube clip cannot give us that experience (so excerpts would probably be upsetting to him).
15. true
16. true

UNIT 15: IMPERIAL RUSSIA—A CULTURAL ODYSSEY

1. Orthodoxy, or Eastern Christianity
2. ortho; right / correct / true; dox/ doxos; carrier of/bearer of
3. a cappella; fluid
4. Old Believers
5. bells
6. icons; worshipped; to look upon with respect and reverence
7. seven; Italian / foreign; Empresses (Tsarinas) Anna, Elizabeth, Catherine the Great
8. Ukrainian; birthplace (original site)
9. Father of Russian Music; it used an important Russian historical story / it had the sound of Russian a cappella church singing, folk rhythms and melodies / it was written at the right time to capture the national mood.
10. serfdom; 1861
11. Chekhov; Seagull, Cherry Orchard, Three Sisters; Stanislavsky; acting
12. The Wanderers, Itinerants, Peredvizhniki; serfs / peasants; aristocracy or royalty; Repin
13. Pushkin; verse; Eugene Onegin; Tatiana; in a duel
14. Tchaikovsky; Mighty Handful (Mighty Five, Mighty Fistful, Moguchaia kuchka); Tchaikovsky; tone poems, Russian operas on historical themes, and anything that would give the flavor of Old Russia
15. Pictures at an Exhibition; Promenade; Baba Yaga; chicken legs
16. Boris Godunov; Riurik; Romanov; guilty conscience, or fear of the murdered Riurik Prince returning; coronation
17. Russian speech (Russian language); mad
18. sailor; orchestrator; St. Petersburg Conservatory; didn't know enough / wasn't qualified to teach; Flight of the Bumblebee
19. son; Igor Stravinsky
20. Rachmaninov; America; a beloved pianist who toured across America.
21. Scriabin; color in music / electricity; a wheel (wooden disc) with colored electric lights to be triggered at different places in his compositions; Bolshevik Revolution; Lenin
22. Ballets russes; Russian dance / exotic ballets; Parisians (the French)
23. Stravinsky; Firebird; puppet; Petrushka; Nijinsky
24. revolutions; February; October; October Revolution / Bolshevik Revolution; Lenin; destroying Russian Christianity / destroying many of the roots of Russian culture

UNIT 16: LOAD UP THE WAGONS: THE STORY OF AMERICAN MUSIC
1. a complete tradition of Native American music already here; oral; genres
2. Regionalism
3. Fiddle tunes; Appalachian
4. 1622; Christianity; reading, writing, singing; Latin
5. Psalmody; Psalms
6. Moravians; North Carolina; organ
7. Shape-note; people were "taught to sing" by traveling singing masters who set up singing schools.
8. Joy to the World; My Faith Looks Up to Thee, When I Survey the Wondrous Cross, Blest Be the Tie That Binds, Nearer My God to Thee
9. March; opera or operetta
10. women / wives/ ladies; husbands; courts, kings, royalty, aristocracy
11. circus
12. Europe
13. George; band master and choir director; know that he composed
14. hymn tunes, melodies from operas and symphonies, march tunes, folk songs, popular songs, etc.; 114 Songs
15. Canadian Army Doctor (and Lieutenant Colonel); red poppy; war dead
16. Mardi gras; that part of America was settled by French Catholics who observed the Liturgical Calendar, and, therefore, held many parties before Lent began; First City / Founding City
17. Chinese; railroads [transcontinental]
18. 1843; Northern; black-face; songs, jokes, tap dancing, tricks, animal acts, and the preferred variety-show format in American entertainment
19. Stephen Foster; O Susanna, Beautiful Dreamer, Camptown Races, I Dream of Jeannie with the Light Brown Hair, etc.; banjo
20. decreased; Vaudeville
21. Irving Berlin; Russia; was not; Alexander's Ragtime Band
22. Ziegfeld; New Amsterdam; Walt Disney Corp.; The Lion King

UNIT 17: TURNING THE PAGE ON WESTERN TRADITION AND THE EXPLOSION OF WAR.
1. fin de siècle; 19th
2. A Nervous Splendor
3. Johannes Brahms, Gustav Mahler, Richard Strauss, Arnold Schönberg, Sigmund Freud, Gustav Klimt, Emperor Franz Joseph
4. Ringstrasse; the huge buildings show wealth, stability, power at a time when much of the social order was crumbling and current events were leading toward World War I.
5. The Scream; Edvard Munch
6. he continued with the traditional "classical" structures inherited from Haydn, Mozart, and Beethoven, writing symphonies, concertos, sonatas, and staying within the musical vocabulary of the Common Practice Era.
7. Beethoven
8. idiomatic

SUGGESTED ANSWERS FOR VIEWING GUIDES

9. Clara Wieck Schumann
10. Jewish; convert to Christianity; Alma (Schindler); quit composing; the death of a little daughter
11. he added many more players to the orchestra. He added vocal soloists and choirs to his symphonies. He used new sounds, including odd percussion (like anvils). He contrasted huge sounds with delicate sounds. He made listeners hear orchestral music in a new way.
12. [the dominance of] German music
13. Impressionist; he was a contemporary of the Impressionist painters / he chose not to write solely in traditional forms, but to create new forms, and paint musical pictures in new sounds, using fluid melody lines, getting rid of a strong pulse, and using a beautiful palate of orchestral sounds; Symbolist; words
14. Impression: Sunrise; Monet; was not
15. waltz
16. chinoiserie; Turandot; Madame Butterfly; stabs (murders); jumps to her death (commits suicide)
17. world's fairs / expositions
18. Richard Strauss; tone poems / symphonic poems; opera conductor; operas; Salome
19. to build little tubes (connected to water bottles) into the "rocks" at the back of the set
20. electricity
21. trekking into remote villages to hear the folksongs; gramophone
22. Romantic; *Verklärte Nacht* (Transfigured Night); atonal / radical / shocking / drastic / bold; did not
23. singing
24. *Rite of Spring*; choreography; Nijinsky; distorted, jagged, against, or the opposite of, Classical ballet technique
25. give it repeated hearings, so that your ear grows and develops, and so that you come to understand and possibly even like it.

Name of work:	Composer:	Composer Dates: /

First Hearing: Simply listen. When you have finished, make a note of what strikes you most about this work. Listen to it again immediately. **Second Hearing:** Answer the following questions:

What is the instrumentation? (treat voice as an instrument)	
Describe the tempo:	
Describe any patterns or repetition that you hear in the music:	
What do you like or dislike about this work?	
Now put the work away and go on to something else. You will come back to it in another listening session soon.	**1st & 2nd Listening Complete Date:**

Third Hearing: Using your notes from the Second Hearing, listen again and think about your answers.

Would you change any of them?	
How do you think this music would have been used when it was first written? For example, is it for dancing, for worship, for use at court, for a concert hall, to be performed at home?	

Listen to the work again immediately (Fourth Hearing).

Fourth Hearing: Answer the following questions:

Describe the texture:	
Do you hear the harmonies? Listen for the harmonic rhythm – how slow or fast the chords change. (This may take practice.) Is it a slow or fast harmonic rhythm?	
Now put the work away and go on to something else. You will come back to this work again. You can listen to it between now and then for enjoyment as often as you wish.	**3rd & 4th Listening Complete Date:**

Fifth Hearing: Review your notes on this piece as you listen to it again.

Do you want to change your prior answers?	
If possible, listen to the work with a teacher, sibling or friend. Tell that person what you think about the work and why. Discuss it.	
Do they agree or disagree with your impressions?	
	5th Listening Complete Date:

Sixth Hearing: Tie this work to another one by answering the following:

What do you like best about this work?	Style?	Instrumentation?	Genre?	Composer?

Based on your answer, look for something not on your Listening Set that you think matches the style, instrumentation, genre, or composer that you like. Search YouTube, Amazon Music, or other service for something similar.

What work did you choose for comparison?	**Title:**	**Composer:**
Does it match your expectation? Do you like it for the same reasons? What surprises you?		
	6th Listening Complete Date:	

| **Name of Work:** | **Composer:** | Page 2 Notes |

Additional Notes re 1st and 2nd Listening:

Additional Notes re 3rd and 4th Listening:

Additional Notes re 5th Listening:

Additional Notes re 6th Listening: